# God's Great Missionaries

## GARY KRAUSE

**Pacific Press® Publishing Association**
Nampa, Idaho
Oshawa, Ontario, Canada
www.pacificpress.com

Cover design by Gerald Lee Monks
Cover illustration by Lars Justinen
Inside Design by Dennis Ferree

Scripture quotations not otherwise credited are from the HOLY BIBLE,
NEW INTERNATIONAL VERSION®, copyright © 1973, 1978, 1984
by the International Bible Society. Used by permission of Zondervan
Bible Publishers.
Scripture quotations marked NLT are taken from the Holy Bible, New
Living Translation, copyright 1996. Used by permission of Tyndale
House Publishers, Inc., Wheaton, Illinois 60189. All rights reserved.
Scriptures quoted from NKJV are from The New King James Version,
copyright © 1979, 1980, 1982, Thomas Nelson, Inc., Publishers.

Additional copies of this book are available by calling toll-free
1-800-765-6955 or online at http://www.adventistbookcenter.com.

Library of Congress Cataloging-in-Publication Data

Krause, Gary, 1962-
God's great missionaries / Gary Krause.
p. cm.
ISBN 13: 978-0-8163-2269-5
ISBN 10: 0-8163-2269-4
1. Seventh-day Adventists—Missions. 2. Missions—Biblical teaching.
3. Evangelistic work—Biblical teaching. I. Title.
BV2495.K73 2008
266'.6732—dc22
2007052301

08 09 10 11 12 • 5 4 3 2 1

# Dedication

For Bettina, my greatly loved wife and best friend.

# Table of Contents

# Preface

I sat in a taxi next to my friend, Pastor Kwon JohngHaeng. He's the Adventist Mission coordinator for northern Asia, which has only a relative handful of Christians among a sands-of-the-sea size population. We discussed the sacrifice of missionaries and the huge mission field facing them. I heard his voice start to break and turned to see him wipe tears from his eyes. As we talked together, I asked myself, *When was the last time I wept for those who don't know Jesus?*

Today I saw a survey in which church members rate the most important goals for their local church. The top five were all about personal spiritual growth and development. Outreach was at the bottom of the list with 12 percent choosing "Work for church growth" and a mere 11 percent indicating "Transform the community" as goals.

What do we really want our church to be? An inward-focusing, spiritual country club for saints? Or Jesus' followers reaching out in His love to people and communities all over the world?

This book draws on the inspiration of men and women in the Bible who pursued life-changing missions for God. As we look at their examples, may we be inspired to help tear down barriers today so we can better see a world in need of Jesus.

I can't blame anyone else for this book, but I want to thank a few for their help and inspiration in so many ways: my wonderful wife,

Bettina; our two-year-old gift from God, Bethany; Bethany's four grandparents and Uncle Wayne; as well as Chris Blake, Andy Nash, Mike Ryan, Global Mission Study Center directors, and the Adventist Mission team.

# CHAPTER 1

# Paul: Sabbath and the Gestapo

Several years ago at a mission emphasis weekend, participants discussed the best ways to present the Christian message in cross-cultural settings. Together we explored ways to build bridges—rather than to put up barriers—to people in other cultures.

On the last day, a man stepped up to the microphone and said, "I've run evangelistic campaigns all around the world, and I've never had to change anything—not even my habit of wearing a suit. You can read the Gospels and never see anywhere that Jesus changed His style of clothes or music when He worked with non-Jewish people."

He was right, at least somewhat. The Gospels don't discuss, in any context, Jesus' dress or choice of music. But did the man overlook the fact that the non-Jewish people Jesus worked with—in Samaria and across the Lake of Galilee in the Gadarene—would have worn the same types of clothes and probably enjoyed similar types of music that Jesus' Jewish compatriots did?

But the bigger point is, of course, that Jesus completely changed the way He presented Himself when He left heaven, came to earth, and became a human being. *That's the greatest example of adaptation for cross-cultural ministry the world has ever seen!*

Today we take for granted that Christianity has spread throughout the world and become the world's largest religion. We forget what a dramatic and revolutionary concept it was for the early church to break from its focus on reaching only Jewish people. It was shocking, like the discovery of gravity, or that the earth moves around the sun. God's salvation appeared for the entire world and not just for Jews.

"It has always been my ambition to preach the gospel where Christ was not known," wrote the apostle Paul (Romans 15:20). As the "apostle to the Gentiles," Paul faced the challenge of proclaiming Jesus as Lord among the idol worshipers, philosophers, and the superstitious throughout the Roman Empire. His approach provides us salient lessons for sharing Jesus with an unbelieving world today.

Paul's background and personality helped equip him as a pioneer missionary. A Roman citizen familiar with both the pagan and Jewish worlds, he was also fluent in Greek. And he served as a missionary when the Roman Empire stretched over the then-known world. His ministry demonstrated that God wasn't limited to expressing Himself through the culture of the Jews. The gospel became a vital message for those immersed in Roman and Greek culture.

Throughout his work as a missionary, Paul faced a barrage of opposition—from inside and outside the church. It's hard to imagine a quiet, shy personality accomplishing what Paul achieved. He was no stranger to disputes. He disagreed sharply with Barnabas over whether to take John Mark on a missionary trip (Acts 15:39). John Mark had earlier deserted Paul, who—though willing to forgive—wasn't ready to forget (Acts 15:37–39).

And yet Paul showed Christian compassion. He lived humbly (1 Corinthians 4:11), without many of life's comforts (2 Corinthians 11:27), and devoted his time and energies to establishing and nurturing new groups of believers. Paul carried a passionate concern for these churches and was jealous to protect them. He treated his new congregations as if they were his own children. He loved them, craved their affection, and worked night and day to strengthen them in their new faith. He regularly wrote them letters and, wherever possible, visited to encourage them.

Paul loved to hear good reports of their faithfulness and their commitment to share God's love. Although he sometimes had to rebuke them, he always did it out of fatherly love and concern.

At times Christians are called to act forcefully for what's right. Even Jesus Himself, with whip in hand, forced the money changers from the temple. Paul wouldn't let anything get in the way of proclaiming the good news.

## Where they were

For more than a hundred years, thousands of Seventh-day Adventist missionaries have followed Paul's example. They've traveled overseas in order to share the love of Jesus with people of many tribes and languages. From Asia to the South Pacific, Africa to the Americas, they've faced the challenge of communicating the good news to people in different cultures. And Adventist missionary pioneers quickly learned that they needed to present themselves and their message in a culturally relevant way.

In 1902 Harry Miller and his wife, Maude, graduated from what is today Loma Linda University. They had no question what they would do next. Both felt a burning call to go to China as medical missionaries.*

Money and prestigious medical careers awaited them in the United States. Harry was such a prodigy that Dr. John Harvey Kellogg tried to persuade them to stay. But they turned their backs on it all to live and work among China's poor.

The Millers traveled with another young physician couple and two nurses. Upon arrival, both Harry Miller and the other male doctor immediately shaved their heads, grew long pigtails, and dressed like the locals.

They didn't learn that in medical school. But they intuitively knew that the more they could be like the people, the more effective they would be. The more cultural barriers they could knock down, the easier for people to accept them. And during Dr. Miller's fifty

* Information in this section on Harry Miller comes from Richard A. Schaefer, *Legacy: Daring to Care,* http://www.llu.edu/info/legacy/Legacy25.html.

years of ministry in China, the Chinese people came to love him dearly.

Miller's impact is hard to underestimate. Clarence Hall, senior editor of *Reader's Digest,* compared Miller with David Livingstone, as one "whose dedicated skills indelibly marked the maps with Christian humanitarianism throughout the world's far places."

It's true that Dr. Miller associated with the elite of Chinese society. He was, for example, friend and physician to the political leader of the Republic of China, General Chiang Kai-Shek, and his wife, Mao. During his time in China, Miller treated nearly every important ruler of China, not to mention ambassadors, senators, and other important persons. But he regarded these accomplishments simply as doorways to greater service—uplifting the underprivileged, feeding the famished, and healing the unfortunate sick. He knew what it was like to live among the people in a "beggar's den"—a three-walled hut open to rain, mosquitoes, and lice. And he often performed surgery in the open fields in order to prevent bugs and leaves falling on his surgical procedures.

Following the example of his Master, Dr. Miller met the people where they were. He lived and worked at their level; he became one with them.

## Maverick

When people take seriously the task of communication, their actions sometimes may seem bizarre or annoying. We can become so comfortable with the way we've always done things that anything different threatens us.

Some years ago I wrote an editorial for the *South Pacific Record* on the need to translate our message into terms that people can understand. I received a letter to the editor from a woman who disagreed. She was a teacher and said that there'd been a fad in education circles of trying to focus on teaching the students as individuals rather than on teaching "the curriculum." She said this experiment had been a disaster because the students weren't learning. The tide, she said, had turned back toward teaching the curriculum.

She made a valid point. In adapting our message to our audience, we must avoid the pitfall of syncretism—where our message becomes so buried in the audience's beliefs and practices that it loses any meaning. We must not sell out our message and become exactly like the people we're trying to reach.

It's folly to water down our doctrine and beliefs in order to accommodate every fad and cultural whim. If we have a mania for "relevance," we'll be forever playing catch-up and be forever irrelevant. Instead of presenting alternatives, we'll be following the world's agenda. And we won't be faithful to God or His Word.

Christianity isn't a political party. We can't achieve our mission just by polling our way, feeding people only what they want to hear and when they want it. If our message is worth believing, it should speak to the culture and not be dictated by it. On the other hand, if we just recite the twenty-eight fundamental beliefs to a Kalahari bushman or a New York stockbroker, we may have taught the curriculum, but we haven't communicated the message.

When we talk of adapting our message to reach people in different contexts, we're not talking about changing or compromising truth. We're not saying that Jesus isn't God or that Wednesday is the Sabbath or that there's an eternal hellfire. We're talking about finding the most effective ways to say that Jesus is God; that the seventh day is the Sabbath; and that when we die, God doesn't suddenly turn into a fire-loving tyrant.

## Sabbath and Gestapo

Several years ago I was studying at a university in Sydney, Australia. Exams approached, and some classmates were talking about the stress of studying all weekend without a break. I told them I always took a twenty-four-hour break on the weekends. I did it for spiritual reasons, but it also made a lot of sense physically. They were shocked. "I might just try that," one of them told me.

My approach wasn't a traditional "here's what the Bible says" approach. I didn't convert my classmates. But I attempted to put the Sabbath at a level to which they could relate. Perhaps it planted a seed. Perhaps it was a starting point.

Was there more to the Sabbath truth than what I told them? Certainly. But not one of my classmates believed the Bible was the Word of God, so I couldn't sit down and give them an in-depth Bible study on the subject. I didn't compromise the truth; I tried to find an "entry level" where it could start to make some sense to them.

C. S. Lewis made a similar point about teaching Christian forgiveness to people in his homeland of England: "If we really want to learn how to forgive, perhaps we had better start with something easier than the Gestapo."* His point was that we need to pace our delivery of the message. Lewis was writing soon after World War II. Memory of the Nazi atrocities still burned in the minds of the British public. Would God's love and forgiveness extend to a repentant member of the Gestapo? Of course. Would this be the best place to begin teaching an English person at that time about God's forgiveness? Of course not.

Pastor Frank Maberly served as a pioneer Adventist missionary among the Enga people of Papua New Guinea. "For three centuries these people had no cultural exchange with other people," says his son, Pastor Clif Maberly. "[My dad] discovered that these people believed in a trinity, and had a shrine for restoring the relation between god and man. They even had an inner holy of holies with two stones, sprinkled with the blood of sacrificed pigs once a year." They also revered ten sacred stones.

Pastor Maberly eagerly related the message of the Bible to familiar cultural practices—using them as an entering wedge to biblical truths.

Paul and other apostles in the early Christian church faced another "problem"—how to incorporate eager-to-learn people from a totally different background who wanted to join their fellowship. The early Christians were, of course, Jews who believed in Jesus, the Messiah. But after a few years, largely because of Paul's work, Gentiles started to take an interest in Christianity.

The apostles convened in Jerusalem to discuss the best way to approach this development. Although we can't access a full tran-

---

* C. S. Lewis, *Mere Christianity* (HarperCollins, 2001), 116.

script of the discussion, Acts 15 does give us a window on what took place.

All the key players were there, including Paul. The apostle James, who was probably Jesus' brother, gave one of the most significant speeches: " 'It is my judgment, therefore, that we should not make it difficult for the Gentiles who are turning to God' " (Acts 15:19).

If James were speaking today, some might accuse him of trying to "water down" the message. But James wasn't suggesting a compromise of truth. He was suggesting—actually, pleading—that the message be meaningful to the culture that they were trying to reach. No unnecessary barriers, please.

## What of the Seventh-day Adventist Church today?

"Christ commissioned His disciples to proclaim a faith and worship that would have in it nothing of caste or country," writes Ellen White, "a faith that would be adapted to all peoples, all nations, all classes of men."*

Imagine one Sabbath arriving at what you think is church. But it's not like any church you've ever seen. There are no walls, no pews, no hymn books. Nobody is wearing a suit. Nobody is wearing a tie. In fact, everyone wears a robe.

There also are no chairs, so you sit on the floor with everybody else, waiting for somebody to get up and give the welcome, prayer, and first hymn. But then suddenly everyone breaks into a chant. It's loud, it's intense, and it's given with great fervor.

After five minutes you wonder how long this will continue. Ten minutes. Twenty minutes. Finally, you turn to your translator to ask what's happening. He explains that they're reciting texts about the greatness of God. Thirty minutes, forty-five minutes—then the worship service is over.

You've just attended "church" with a new Global Mission group in a country in Southeast Asia. No sermon. No hymns. And yet, the service made the message of Scripture meaningful and relevant to people within their culture.

---

* *The Desire of Ages,* 820.

Some years ago I was in the country of Burkina Faso, in West Africa, with Mike Ryan, who was then director of Global Mission for the world church. Mike has a passion for church planting and making sure it's done well. We were visiting a Global Mission pioneer and his congregation of new believers, and I took out a video camera to capture the worship service. They started to sing, but they were singing a western hymn, awkwardly, uncomfortably; to be frank, they were kind of limping along.

Mike quietly walked over to the pioneer and whispered in his ear. The pioneer smiled broadly, stopped his church members, and spoke to them in the local language. They started up again—this time meaningfully praising God with a drum and clapping in joyful, tuneful, and rhythmic music.

In both these scenarios God was being honored. God's Word carries a timeless application across cultural boundaries. His message doesn't need a cultural passport or visa. He speaks to people where they are, within the parameters of their experience.

Naturally each of us feels more comfortable with certain cultural expressions. But we can't allow our personal tastes or preferences to dictate the way our message is shared. We must reach people where they are, in words and actions they can understand and appreciate.

I'll never forget talking to the senior elder at a church I attended. An older man nearing retirement, he told me he didn't much care for the newer songs sung during worship services. His preference was traditional hymns. "But, Gary, I can see how it is ministering to the young people," he said. "And if my two boys had attended a church like this, they may never have left the Seventh-day Adventist Church."

Somehow I think that senior elder and the apostle Paul would have been good friends.

# CHAPTER 2

# Paul: Dressing the Christian Message

Medical missionary Paul White tells the parable of Grogi, the sick monkey, who was being treated by Pilli, the studious monkey. Pilli was studying the book *Medicines and First Aid for Monkeys and Others*. He took a bandage from his black bag and bound Grogi's leg exactly as the book said. Throughout the procedure Grogi couldn't stop coughing and shivering.

Twiga, the giraffe, watched the procedure and asked, "Can't you do something for his cough, Pilli?"

"Can shivering be splintered or a cough bandaged?" Pilli scoffed.

"The whole of health is not wrapped in bandages," warned Twiga.

The next day Pilli returned to work on Grogi's legs.

"Oh, monkey," said Twiga the giraffe, "do you not think medicines might be found to bring peace and comfort to the chest of your relation?"

Pilli wasn't impressed, stared coldly at the giraffe, muttered something, and continued with his bandaging.

Several days later Grogi was dead. Pilli was angry.

"This cannot be so," he said. "I bandaged his legs daily with skill."

Twiga commented, sadly: "Might it be that bandaging a leg is not the best treatment for . . . pneumonia?"*

---

* Paul White, Jungle Doctor Fables, http://www.sarahsministry.org.

17

## Dressing the message

Effective outreach matches the medicine to the need. A starving person's first priority won't be a lecture on Daniel. A Thai Buddhist won't be overly interested in why Saturday rather than Sunday is the Sabbath. An atheist investment banker in New York City won't suddenly believe in God if we read her twenty Bible proof texts. We must make sure that our methods reach the people where they are.

Ellen White says it well: "[The apostle Paul] varied his manner of labor, shaping his message to the circumstances under which he was placed." She adds, "The laborer for God [should] . . . study carefully the best methods . . ." and "[Christians] are not to be one-idea men, stereotyped in their manner of working, unable to see that their advocacy of truth must vary with the class of people among whom they work and the circumstances they have to meet."*

People who study mission call this process "contextualization," which means dressing the Christian message in clothes appropriate to a particular culture or people. In other words, we translate the message into concepts and actions that make sense to those we are trying to reach. And to do this, we must understand the specific culture.

Cultures aren't exotic phenomena found only in the pages of *National Geographic* magazine. A culture may range from Islamic Sharia Law in northern Nigeria to your neighborhood Rotary Club to a group of teenage skateboarders down the road. Most Christians agree that overseas missionaries need to learn the cultural nuances of the people with whom they're working. But are we aware of the different cultures in our own street?

As I took groceries out of our car one day, I overheard a group of neighborhood kids talking across the road.

"My grandfather was one hundred, smoked one cigarette, and then he died."

"What happens when people die?"

"When I die, I'm going to heaven."

"Nobody knows where we go when we die. Not even dead people."

---

* *Gospel Workers*, 300, 119.

# Paul: Dressing the Christian Message

"Have any of you seen ghosts?"

"I saw a movie where . . ."

"Do spirits live forever?"

On our street live Blacks and Whites, Indians, Vietnamese, Brazilians, Mexicans—and others I don't know. There are Protestants, Catholics, Hindus, Muslims, and nonbelievers. There are singles, couples with no children, and families. Young and old. Just hearing those children talk reminded me again of the diversity of backgrounds and worldviews in our one street. And it reminded me again that there's no one-size-fits-all approach to outreach, even in my own neighborhood.

In our digital world, so many worldviews collide and compete. Type a few words on an Internet search engine, and you'll find hundreds of contradictory views about religion, spirituality, and God. Switch on a television, listen to the radio, or read a newspaper, and you'll find even more.

Even the movies have spiritual perspectives. "Hollywood has done something remarkable: It has created a great and very successful religion," writes Rabbi Adin Steinsaltz. "Through its successful missionaries—the films produced in Hollywood—it has spread around the globe, gaining adherents faster than any other religion in the world. If it has not attained the stature of a full-fledged religion, at least it is a very strong cult."*

If the apostle Paul were alive today, how would he vary his manner of labor? How would he shape his message? Instead of quoting pagan poets on Mars' Hill, would he be dissecting films on CNN?

Are we Seventh-day Adventists studying carefully "the best methods"? Do we see clearly that our advocacy of truth has to vary with the type of people we're working with and the circumstances we face?

For centuries most Christians have tried to share God's love in the language of the people they're talking to. But some denominations

---

* Adin Steinsaltz, quoted in Dick Staub, *The Culturally Savvy Christian* (San Francisco: John Wiley & Sons, 2007), 17.

still conduct services in a language the vast majority of their members can't understand.

At a church I visited in the Middle East, I couldn't understand a word of the liturgy but took comfort in the fact that neither could any of the locals. As I sat, I made the unwitting grievous mistake of crossing my legs, only to have one of the priests stop, stare, and shake his finger at me. At no time was any effort made to make the service meaningful for a visitor or to communicate in the language of the listener.

When the apostle Paul was arrested in Jerusalem, a violent crowd yelled, "Kill him, kill him!" When he finally got to speak to them, he spoke in Aramaic—the local language. The Bible says that when they heard him speak in their own language, they became silent (Acts 21:33–22:2). Something powerful occurs when we hear a message in our own language.

But we need to go further. For example, let's say that we translate a set of Bible study reading guides, designed for English-speaking Americans, into the Thai language. Great! Now Thai people will have the opportunity to read our beliefs in their own language. But will they really?

No. To start with, a Thai won't understand many of the illustrations and stories in the American guides. The guides will present ideas in a teaching/propositional style that may not suit a Thai reader. They'll also make assumptions that aren't necessarily true; for example, they may assume that a Thai person has a concept of a personal God and has knowledge of the Bible.

An effective approach to Thai people will require more than just translating existing materials into the Thai language and inserting a few pictures of Thai people. Effective communication requires prayer, an understanding of their current spiritual thought patterns, and a willingness to interact with them in new ways. In other words, we have to get "inside" their heads and hearts.

The messages of Scripture were written at specific times, in specific places, within specific cultural frameworks. And yet, their themes are timeless and speak to people in all cultures today; that is, if presented in the right way.

We can't afford to ignore local contexts. I can produce a high quality DVD of evangelistic sermons covering the twenty-eight fundamental beliefs of Seventh-day Adventists, preached in English by a Western evangelist. However, if I take this DVD to China, I can't insert it in a standard DVD player and watch it. The DVD is in a Region 1 coding, while in China they use Region 3 coding. The message will be garbled.

In the same way I can put a standard witnessing package together—add doctrines, mix in some Bible verses, and then pass it on to someone in a different culture. There may be nothing wrong with the package and what it contains. But for communication to be effective, the recipients have to understand and assimilate what they've been given.

*How are we going to translate the package without watering it down or changing the message?* Will we translate it in a way that people will understand?

## Removing barriers

The apostle Paul wanted to remove all possible barriers to the gospel so that he could reach as many people as possible. That's why it pained him to see Jewish Christians erecting barriers for non-Jewish believers. Unchecked, these Jewish believers could create a major roadblock to his mission to the Gentiles. The Council at Jerusalem had been a milestone in the growth of the Christian church; it provided an entry point for Gentiles without requiring them to practice Jewish customs that weren't binding on non-Jews. And the last thing the infant church needed was Jewish Christians telling new Gentile believers that they had to abide by regulations that weren't tests of fellowship.

At one point Paul became furious with those who said circumcision was required. He said that he wished they'd go all the way and castrate themselves (Galatians 5:12). Although this sounds crude, it shows how strongly the apostle rejected anything that would make it hard for unbelievers to join the church. The apostle James had said it so well at the Council in Jerusalem: " 'It is my judgment, therefore, that we should not make it difficult for the Gentiles who are turning to God' " (Acts 15:19). And now Paul could see people making it difficult again.

So why did Paul, immediately after the Council at Jerusalem, advise Timothy to be circumcised before going on a missionary journey to Derbe and Lystra? "In deference to the Jews of the area," writes Luke, "he arranged for Timothy to be circumcised before they left, for everyone knew that his father was a Greek" (Acts 16:3, NLT).

Paul was merely applying his own principle of being "all things to all men" (1 Corinthians 9:22). He opposed circumcision as a requirement for salvation, but if it would break down prejudice and open up paths for the gospel, he'd do it. You get the idea that Paul would have cut off his own hand if it would lead someone to Jesus.

## One voice among many

Today, most postmodern people don't look to organized religion as a major authority. Other factors play a larger role, and for them Christianity is merely one voice among many.

In fact, many people not only don't believe the Bible, they know nothing about it. They're not concerned whether something is right or wrong according to the Bible. They don't care about theology or "truth." They don't worry whether Saturday or Sunday is the correct Sabbath. They've never kept any day "holy." They don't worry whether life starts after death or after the resurrection. They first need to be convinced that there *is* life after death. How do we build bridges to them? How do we even begin to share the good news in a relevant way?

Paul wrote to the Corinthians, "Though I am free and belong to no man, I make myself a slave to everyone, to win as many as possible. To the Jews I became like a Jew, to win the Jews. . . . To the weak I became weak, to win the weak. I have become all things to all men so that by all possible means I might save some" (1 Corinthians 9:19–22).

This is a baffling text. What does it mean to "become all things to all people"?

A religious sect called The Family used to be known as the Children of God. Perhaps their most infamous practice was "Flirty Fishing." Founder and leader David Berg encouraged his women followers to have "loving sex" with men as a way of leading them to God.

They officially stopped using this unique witnessing technique in 1987. But a few years ago I asked the media spokesperson for The Family in Australia about it, and he defended it. In fact, The Family's Web site still makes no apologies: "In 1976, David proposed an unprecedented corollary to the Law of Love: He contended that, in certain circumstances, it would be acceptable for a Christian to have sexual relations with someone in an effort to demonstrate a tangible manifestation of God's love, thereby helping them to come to a saving knowledge of Jesus Christ. This doctrine became known as 'Flirty Fishing,' a term that David [Berg] adapted from Jesus' admonition to His disciples to 'follow Me, and I will make you fishers of men' (Matthew 4:19). It was practiced by many Family members until 1987, when it was discontinued, largely due to the need to spend more time in other forms of outreach."*

Let's be clear. Whatever Paul was advocating in his letter to the Corinthians, it wasn't that we should change ethics, doctrines, or any of the truth Jesus presented. Paul was talking about dressing truth in different clothes for different cultures in order to make it more meaningful and understandable. And he modeled this in his own ministry.

## To the Jews

In the book of Acts we find a distinct pattern Paul followed when ministering to Jews and to those who "feared God" (God-fearing non-Jewish believers worshiped in synagogues). It was Paul's habit to enter a city, visit the synagogue, teach the good news, and reason from the Scriptures (see, for example, Acts 17:1–3).

On one occasion Paul and Barnabas visited the port town of Perga, in modern-day Turkey. As usual, on Sabbath morning they attended the synagogue. After the services—including readings from the books of Moses and the Prophets—the synagogue leaders extended an invitation for the visitors to share some thoughts.

---

* "Flirty Fishing," http://www.thefamily.org/ourfounder/tribute/trib_21.htm.

Paul stood to speak. He began his sermon with the Exodus, moved through a history of Israel to the time of King David, introduced the Messianic promise, and connected it to Jesus. He showed that all Scripture points to Jesus.

Paul's method of using Scriptures worked because his audience shared his belief in the Bible's inspiration. They had a common text, and Paul interpreted this text in order to point them to Jesus. Paul "became a Jew"—which wasn't hard since he was a Jew—to reach the Jews.

But this approach would never have worked with the pagans.

## To the pagans

After ministering to the Jews in Perga and then in Iconium (and as usual, stirring up riots in both places), Paul and Barnabas went to the pagan city of Lystra. On its outskirts stood a temple to the Greek god Zeus.

While Paul was preaching, he noticed a cripple and immediately healed him. The people were astonished, and they began shouting in their own dialect, " 'These men are gods in human form!' " (Acts 14:11, NLT). They decided that Paul, the main speaker, must be Hermes, and Barnabas must be the Greek god Zeus.

Not knowing the local dialect, Paul and Barnabas probably had no idea what the people were saying. But when the temple priest and the crowd brought oxen and wreaths of flowers to the city gates in order to sacrifice to the two of them, they "tore their clothes" (Acts 14:14).

They ran out among the people and exclaimed, " 'Men, why are you doing this?' " (Acts 14:15). Then Paul told them the gospel story but with an approach far different from how he had spoken to the Jews in Lystra, " 'We are merely human beings—just like you! We have come to bring you the Good News that you should turn from these worthless things and turn to the living God, who made heaven and earth, the sea, and everything in them. In the past he permitted all the nations to go their own ways, but he never left them without evidence of himself and his goodness. For instance, he sends you rain and good crops and gives you food and joyful hearts' " (Acts 14:15–17, NLT).

# Paul: Dressing the Christian Message

Notice how Paul doesn't appeal to Scripture. His audience had probably never heard of these writings. So Paul turns to something that they do share in common—the world in which they live. He builds on this to talk about a Creator, and contrasts Him with their useless idols. Paul does refer to Scripture in verse 15, but only as he would quote any piece of literature. He doesn't use it as an authority.

On another occasion, when in Athens, Paul preached to the Jewish people in the synagogue on the Sabbath and to the pagans in the marketplace during the week. The Greek culture Paul witnessed in Athens was far removed from the Jewish culture that was his heritage. Home to the great Greek philosophers Socrates, Aristotle, and Plato, Athens had a legacy of learning and philosophy that was still strong. One day some Stoic and Epicurean philosophers invited him to present his teaching at the Areopagus on Mars' Hill.

Paul began by noting that the people of Athens were very religious, and he referred to their statue to the unknown god. He began his speech on "their turf." He then quoted some of their own poetry—"In Him we live and move and have our being"—which is from *De Oraculis,* written by a seventh century B.C. Cretan poet named Epimenides. And he quotes "we are his offspring" from *The Phenomena,* written in the third century B.C. by Aratus.*

Again Paul looks to the common ground of nature and from there makes a connection to the supernatural.†

---

* Acts 17:22–28.

† Some interpret Ellen White as saying the apostle Paul later regretted his approach on Mars' Hill. (For example, she says, "As he thought of the time thus spent, and realized that his teaching in Athens had been productive of but little fruit, he decided to follow another plan of labor in Corinth."—*The Acts of the Apostles,* 244.) But such statements must be seen in the light of other comments she makes about Paul on Mars' Hill:

1. God spoke through Paul.
2. He gained a victory for Christianity in the heart of paganism (p. 240).
3. The words he spoke "contain a treasure of knowledge for the church" (p. 241).
4. He spoke with "a tact born of divine love" (p. 241).
5. He ably "exposed the fallacies of the religion of the Athenians" (p. 237).

Paul may have fine-tuned his approach later in Corinth, but it didn't negate how God led him to speak on Mars' Hill.

Paul made history as he defended Christianity against the tide of paganism in Athens. Compromise was the last thing on his mind. Extremely learned in Judaism, Paul had sat at the feet of Gamaliel, one of the greatest Jewish teachers. He understood the Torah. He was steeped in a religion that detested idols. His conversion to become a follower of Jesus reinforced his faith in the One true God and his abhorrence of anything that sought to take His place.

At no stage does "becoming all things to all people" on Mars' Hill involve Paul compromising the truth. Rather, this method allowed him to preach the truth in words his audience could understand. It led him to quote from the popular culture, from poets and writers with whom his audience were familiar. Of course, Paul was following the loving example of Jesus, who also spoke to people in ways they could understand. Today we need to find ways to get the message to where people are. That means genuinely listening to them, focusing on their needs and interests, and shaping our message in a way that connects with them.

It means we must treat the coughing with medicine, not bandages.

# CHAPTER 3

# John the Baptist:
# A Little Subversion

A few years ago, the official Harley-Davidson motorcycle Web site carried a picture of a bearded baby boomer in jeans and leather jacket joyfully astride a Harley. The caption read: "Suppose time takes a picture—one picture that represents your entire life here on earth. You have to ask yourself how you'd rather be remembered. As a pasty, web-wired computer wiz, strapped to an office chair? Or as a leather-clad adventurer who lived life to the fullest astride a Harley-Davidson? You can decide which it is, but think quickly. Time is framing up that picture, and it's got a pretty itchy shutter finger."

Have you ever thought of Christians as adventurers? How will the itchy shutter finger of time remember us? As pasty Christians strapped to ritual and "we've always done it this way before"? Or as Christian adventurers who lived life to the fullest—not riding a motorcycle but following where an adventurous God led? Time is framing up that picture right now.

## John the adventurer

In an important sense, John the Baptist was more like an exuber-ant Harley rider than someone bound to an office chair. He endured ridicule, persecution, depression, and martyrdom. But John was on a nonstop adventure for God, and Jesus praised him as the greatest man ever born (Matthew 11:11).

From the beginning, John was destined to be different. His life resulted from a miraculous pregnancy, and his parents dedicated him to God for a specific task. Old and childless, his mother shouted with joy when she learned she was pregnant. Appropriately, the name John—*Ioannes* in Greek—means "Jehovah is a gracious giver" or "Yahweh has mercy."

There was a fervent expectation that the son of Elizabeth and Zechariah would accomplish wonderful things. The angel who appeared to Zechariah informed him that his son would " 'be a joy and delight to you' " and " 'many will rejoice because of his birth' " (Luke 1:14).

When the angel told an astonished Zechariah that he would have a son, Zechariah couldn't believe it. In response, the angel struck him dumb. That has always sounded a bit tough to me. Given the circumstances, who wouldn't find the announcement hard to believe? But we're not told why he was silenced. Perhaps God thought it was such an important time that any word of dissent, any negative feelings, would spoil the sacred occasion. We just don't know.

After he regained speech, Zechariah was filled with the Holy Spirit and prophesied. No wonder Luke records that "the neighbors were all filled with awe" and "throughout the hill country of Judea people were talking about all these things" (Luke 1:65). No wonder everyone wondered, " 'What then is this child going to be?' " (verse 66).

Few people in the Bible started with such a spectacular calling or such high expectations. Perhaps the closest parallel is with Jesus, John's first cousin, whose birth was also accompanied by angels and visions.

## Preparing the way

Centuries earlier Isaiah prophesied about "A voice of one calling: 'In the desert prepare the way for the Lord; make straight in the wilderness a highway for our God' " (Isaiah 40:3).

Matthew, Luke, and John all apply these words to John the Baptist. "Prepare the way" suggests clearing obstructions from a road.

The imagery echoes the custom of sending engineers ahead to prepare the road for a visiting king. Isaiah describes raising valleys, lowering hills, and leveling rough ground—constructing a "highway" on which the king could safely and comfortably travel (Isaiah 40:4).

Today when dignitaries travel, we see a similar process. The president of the United States, for example, always sends personnel ahead to check security and make sure all protocols and arrangements are set in place before he visits. And when he arrives, flashing cars, police, and security details clear the way.

John's calling was the highest of all callings: to prepare people for the coming King of kings. But like the prophets before him, he wasn't called to a life of ease. Once when Jesus was teaching the crowds, He asked them about John the Baptist: " 'What did you go out to see? A man dressed in fine clothes? No, those who wear expensive clothes and indulge in luxury are in palaces' " (Luke 7:25). When John went out preaching and baptizing by the Jordan River, he wasn't offered reservations at the Jordan River Ritz-Carlton. He wore rough garments of camel's hair and ate locusts and honey.

The teachers of the Law at the time of Jesus taught that Elijah would return and restore " 'all things' " before the Messiah appeared (Mark 9:11–13). Likewise, the prophet Malachi predicted that Elijah would return before the " 'day of the Lord' " (Malachi 4:5, 6).

John the Baptist was the Elijah of his day. Like Elijah, John preached a message of judgment and repentance. Like Elijah and the other Old Testament prophets, John didn't preach a soothing message to comfort his listeners. He didn't congratulate people on their goodness; rather, he chastised them for their wickedness.

John told people how to change their lives (Luke 3:10–14), and his concerns echoed those of the prophets before him. They should share food and clothing with those in need (verse 11); tax collectors shouldn't cheat their clients (verse 13); soldiers shouldn't extort money or falsely accuse people (verse 14).

Like Jesus, John kept his most scathing words for the religious leaders. He called the Pharisees and Sadducees a " 'brood of

29

vipers' " (Matthew 3:7). Not the kind of language to win friends and gain perks, to be sure. He told leaders that their proud boast of being Abraham's children meant nothing. Rather than clinging to tradition, they needed to " 'produce fruit in keeping with repentance' " (Matthew 3:8) because any tree that didn't produce good fruit would be cut down and burned (Matthew 3:10).

The people flocked to hear John; his message delighted them. But his prophetic voice led to his death. Unafraid to stand up even against the political rulers, he told the leader that marrying his sister-in-law Herodias (Matthew 14:4) was a sin. Herod was so angry he wanted to lynch John on the spot, but he feared the people, who loved John.

Herodias hated John. "So Herodias nursed a grudge against John and wanted to kill him"(Mark 6:19). Finally, she obtained her wish when she persuaded her dancing daughter to ask the drunken and debauched Herod for John's head (Matthew 14:6–11).

What a contrast: the highly principled and disciplined life of the prophet versus the king's supreme lack of self-control. One lived in poverty, the other in wealth. One was a spiritual billionaire, the other spiritually bankrupt.

## The subversive mission

A few years ago the *Washington Post* ran an article which said that at one time the Seventh-day Adventist Church was "considered a little subversive."* I stopped and reread that line. *Us? Subversive?* I checked the dictionary to make sure I hadn't misunderstood. It defined subversive as "undermining the established way of doing things." Not a bad word to describe a movement with a prophetic message like Elijah's and John the Baptist's.

The article went on to say that the presence of the Adventist world headquarters in Takoma Park, Maryland, "contributed to the city's progressive reputation." That, too, made me stand a little taller. The article referred to the fact that the Adventist Church was prominent in promoting vegetarianism and that we opposed smok-

---

* *Washington Post*, April 16, 1999.

ing and drinking alcohol. That's when it added that we were "considered a little subversive."

Really? Today, at least in the West, we're often about as subversive as Marines on parade. We're solid citizens. We tend to be middle-class, politically conservative, private-school educated, living in the suburbs, good neighbors. We're law-abiding, sincere, family minded, caring, upright—and we keep our tidy lawns.

But historically, it's true—we've been subversive. We often undercut the established and accepted way of doing things. Our pioneers weren't only health reformers; they were antiwar. Adventist publications were banned from slave states during the American Civil War because of their antislavery attitudes. In an entry on Florence Keller, an Adventist missionary to New Zealand in the early 1900s, the *Dictionary of New Zealand Biography* says, "Adventists were progressive in their attitudes toward women."* Get out the Adventist history books, and you'll see the range of issues where we subverted the status quo. We even subverted women's clothes. Ellen White was an antifashion designer of the reform dress—a far more practical and healthful alternative to the fashions that society was literally squeezing women into.

But are we starting to lose our edge, our distinctiveness? We're not so peculiar anymore. It's politically correct not to smoke; vegetarian food is fashionable in many places; non-Adventist students flock to highly respected Adventist schools around the world; and refusing alcoholic drinks at parties hardly raises an eyebrow.

As Adventists we've also taught a radical theology—including a seventh-day Sabbath and a hell without permanent flames. These were subversive doctrines. I remember as a kid listening to an energetic Adventist public evangelist tell "war stories" from when he publicly debated religious leaders in towns throughout Australia and New Zealand. I was enthralled as he paced back and forth on

---

* Fiona McKergow, "Keller, Nettie Florence 1875-1974," *Dictionary of New Zealand Biography,* updated June 22, 2007, http://www.dnzb.govt.nz.

the church rostrum like a prize fighter, describing the debates as if they were boxing matches.

But today even some of these beliefs are coming in from the cold. Not so long ago, *Christianity Today,* the flagship evangelical publication, carried an article featuring the growing number of evangelical theologians who don't believe in eternal hellfire. And a plethora of books now promote the subject of Sabbath keeping. They're from secular publishers who have flooded stores with books such as *Sabbath: Restoring the Sacred Rhythm of Rest* and *A Day of Rest: Creating a Spiritual Space in Your Week.* What's going on?

I can also remember sitting riveted to my seat as a kid, as I listened to "real, live" missionaries from "the islands" telling miracle stories and pioneering tales. By choosing to become missionaries, they undercut the values of their materialistic society. They left the comforts, security, and predictability of their "homelands" because they were on fire with a mission to change lives for Jesus.

Now, mission stories aren't so popular. It's a shame, because our mission challenge is great. Look at the huge populations in the 10/40 Window—stretching from northwest Africa through the Middle East and into Asia—who've never even heard the name of Jesus. Look at the growing numbers of unbelievers in the secular and postmodern West. Perhaps we feel the pressure of a society that frowns on converting people, a society that preaches a postmodern gospel of acceptance of all beliefs. Perhaps we've lost sight of the vital, transforming power of Jesus. We've forgotten how the gospel story at its root is totally subversive—overturning prejudices, making the weak strong, changing lives.

Rather than being subversive in the West, we generally live comfortably. We polished off our rough edges; many of our quirks have even become mainstream. We once led antitobacco campaigns, but appear to have lost the war against alcohol. Years ago savvy alcohol executives saw what was happening to the cigarette industry and enlisted the help of Madison Avenue marketers and advertisers. They started promoting "responsible," moderate drinking (kind of like healthy smoking and therapeutic sky diving without a parachute). Emerging like the good guys, they hijacked the debate and muzzled our voice.

And most of the new Sabbath books, which aren't written by Adventists, promote the spiritual benefits of keeping a sabbath—but not the seventh-day Sabbath.* What other opportunities have we missed?

As Adventists we haven't completely lost our subversive impulse, but have we become too safe? Do we treasure respectability too much? Have we lost our energy, our enthusiasm, our vision? Have we stopped subverting "the pattern of this world" (Romans 12:2)? Given what we've known for more than a hundred and fifty years, why haven't we been writing bridge-building books on the Sabbath and other topics? Why haven't we tackled the myth-spinning beer manufacturers? Why aren't we known as friends of the poor? In what ways could we now be seen as progressive, cutting-edge, subversive Christians?

The Christian message is ultimately subversive—"This world is not my home." And the Adventist message is an Elijah message. It's a John the Baptist message. But while we're still here, strangers in a strange land, Jesus has instructed us to be "wise as serpents, and harmless as doves" (Matthew 10:16, KJV). A truly Christian subversion is wise and loving. An authentic prophetic voice is both critical and compassionate.

Although John the Baptist didn't hire a public-relations firm to give his message a positive spin, there's no virtue in stirring up animosity. At times Adventist aggression has lost us friends. At times, too, doctrinal snobbery has alienated our neighbors. Love must motivate all we do. The early Christian church was subversive, yet it enjoyed "the favor of all the people" (Acts 2:44–47). At least for a while.

It's not too late to become "a little subversive" again. And we can still keep tidy lawns.

---

* This is one of the many good things about my friend Chris Blake's book *Searching for a God to Love*. It's published by Word Books, a non-Adventist publisher, as well as by Pacific Press®, and eloquently testifies to the importance of the seventh-day Sabbath and other core Adventist beliefs.

## Facing life honestly

Prophets are human. Elijah and John the Baptist, both mighty men of God, at times doubted and questioned their mission. Elijah enjoyed a literal mountaintop experience when he contested with the prophets of Baal on Mount Carmel. He reveled in every minute of it, mocking unmercifully the pagan prophets as their gods proved powerless (1 Kings 18:16–45).

But after he came down from the mountain, he descended to the valley—he was tired, hungry, lonely, discouraged. He lay under a juniper tree and begged God to let him die (1 Kings 19:4).

And John, too, went through a season of doubt. Alone in jail, John let worries and doubts haunt his mind. John, who had known nothing but the freedom of open spaces, of living in the wilderness, was now confined and shackled. Such treatment has sent lesser people to madness. So John sent his disciples to Jesus, seeking assurance that He really was the Messiah.

I suspect it was like driving to work with a lingering worry that you forgot to turn off the kitchen stove. You're sure you did, but you're not willing to bet your life on it. And so you turn around and go home to check. John was sure Jesus was the Messiah, but he sent his disciples just to be sure.

John was in a fragile condition. The last thing he needed was a lecture on his lack of faith. Jesus responded lovingly, gently, " 'Go back and report to John what you hear and see: The blind receive sight, the lame walk, those who have leprosy are cured, the deaf hear, the dead are raised, and the good news is preached to the poor' " (Matthew 11:4, 5).

These words were soothing balm to John. It was happening. Everything he'd lived for, preached for, prayed for. In his damp prison cell, conviction grabbed him. It had been worth it all.

James Appel, a young Adventist missionary doctor and administrator of Hôpital Adventiste de Béré in Chad, knows discouragement. Chad is one of the poorest countries in the world, and Dr. Appel and his wife, Sarah, face a daily battle to find the necessary resources to run this Adventist hospital. He writes, "To say that things are always rosy, exciting and rewarding here would be a lie. . . .

We live in a world that is full of doubts, fears, rejection, disappointment and disillusionment. That is what living in this world is . . . no matter where we are. But that doesn't mean God doesn't also fill up each day with visions and reminders of how things are supposed to be. It doesn't mean that I am not satisfied to the core. It doesn't mean I'm not at peace. *Au contraire,* I can say that not a day goes by that I don't humbly thank God for bringing me here."*

He adds, "*When* you're at the depths of frustration and hopelessness not knowing where to start, or when you're at the heights of saving lives dramatically, touching someone, feeling God's presence in a vibrant way—at any and all of these points you are living, really living."

Even Mother Teresa, long revered for her selfless work among the poor of Calcutta, had a dark night of the soul that *Time* magazine, in a cover article, suggests may have lasted fifty years. On one occasion she wrote a prayer: "I call, I cling, I want—and there is no One to answer—no One on Whom I can cling—no, No One.—Alone . . . Where is my Faith—even deep down right in there is nothing, but emptiness & darkness—My God—how painful is this unknown pain—I have no Faith—I dare not utter the words & thoughts that crowd in my heart—& make me suffer untold agony."†

John the Baptist may have been the greatest man born of a woman. He may have been a powerful prophet and friend. He may have been a tremendous evangelist. But he was still human, still subject to fluctuations of mood and brain chemistry as is everyone else.

Too often our mission stories feature only happy endings. We praise God for stories that end well, but let's not ignore the realities: Global Mission pioneers sometimes get beaten; missionaries get killed; our mission budgets stretch past their limits; at times misguided zeal gets in the way of the gospel.

Like John the Baptist, we need to face life honestly. It's appropriate for God's friends to ask hard questions—even of Jesus.

---

* James Appel, "Don't Worry," blog entry March 5, 2004, at http://bereadventisthospital.blogspot.com.

† David Van Biema, "Her Agony," *Time,* September 3, 2007, 17.

# Jesus: Balancing Actions and Words

My good friend Chris Blake proposes fifteen "amendments," or additions, to the baptismal vows of the Seventh-day Adventist Church. Chris values brevity and focus, so if he's adding things, they're probably important. One of these "extras" says, "I will involve myself in risky, godly sharing. At times, I will move outside my comfort zone to spread the good news about Jesus. If necessary, I'll use words."*

This thought echoes a statement widely attributed to the medieval Italian mystic Francis of Assisi: "Go and preach the gospel. If necessary, use words." There's no evidence that Saint Francis actually made this statement, but it certainly fits the spirit of his teachings. He even instructed his friars not to preach without permission. Then he added, "Let all the brothers, however, preach by their deeds."†

A parallel thought comes out of Jewish tradition. The story goes that a non-Jew came to Shammai, a leading Jewish scholar of the first century, whose words are recorded in the Mishnah. In theology, Shammai opposed Hillel, another leading scholar of the

---

* Chris Blake, *Swimming Against the Current* (Nampa, Idaho: Pacific Press® Publishing Association, 2007), 231.
† Chapter XVII of his Rule of 1221.

day. The Gentile asked Shammai to teach him the entire Torah, but to do it in the time it took to stand on one foot. Shammai was offended at such blasphemy and chased the Gentile away with a stick.

After being rebuffed so strongly, the Gentile came to Hillel and asked him the same thing. Hillel treated the request seriously and took no offense. "What is hateful to you, do not to your fellow man," he said. "This is the entire Torah. All the rest is commentary—now go and study."*

Jesus reflects Hillel's view when He instructs His disciples, " 'So in everything, do to others what you would have them do to you, for this sums up the Law and the Prophets' " (Matthew 7:12). Later the apostle Paul said, "The entire law is summed up in a single command: 'Love your neighbor as yourself' " (Galatians 5:14). The apostle James calls this "the royal law" (James 2:8).

Here Jesus, Paul, and James summarize the meaning of Scripture, not in terms of a theological idea but as an action—something we must do.

## Actions speak louder . . .

Henri Nouwen, writer, theologian, and academic, held prestigious teaching and research posts at Yale University, University of Notre Dame, the Menninger Foundation, and Harvard University. He was a prolific and highly respected writer on many topics, but his writings on spirituality are perhaps the most appreciated. His life revolved around words, but those weren't enough for him.

Throughout his career Nouwen looked for ways to help the poor and oppressed. In the 1960s he joined Martin Luther King's civil rights movement. At one time he even traveled to South America to see if he could serve as a missionary.

Finally he quit academia and went to work for the Daybreak Community in Toronto, Canada—spending the last ten years of

---

* Quoted in William C. Varner, "Jesus and the Pharisees: A Jewish Perspective," http://www.pfo.org/pharisee.htm.

his life caring for six mentally handicapped children, helping meet their daily needs, showing them the compassion of Jesus.

Author Philip Yancey recalls having dinner with a group of Christian writers, including Richard Foster and Eugene Peterson. At one stage Foster and Peterson mentioned "an intense young man" who had asked them both for spiritual help. Foster and Peterson wrote back, suggesting reading materials that might help him spiritually. Foster had just heard that the same young man also contacted Nouwen. "You won't believe what Nouwen did," said Foster. "He invited this stranger to live with him for a month so he could mentor him in person."*

C. S. Lewis, despite heavy demands on his time as a famous author and academic, personally responded to each of the thousands of letters he received. He often prayed for people who wrote to him and would welcome walk-up visitors into his home and even serve them refreshments. Lewis also provided scholarships for many students who couldn't afford an education. During World War II, he opened up his home to children in need. On one occasion, a mentally disabled teenager stayed in his home for three months. After teaching elite students at Oxford University during the day, he would come home and help this troubled boy learn how to read.†

A central theme of Jesus' teaching is to let our lives testify to the glory of God. In the Sermon on the Mount, Jesus describes His followers as " 'the light of the world' " that should never be shrouded or hidden. " 'In the same way,' " He says, " 'let your light shine before men, that they may see your good deeds and praise your Father in heaven' " (Matthew 5:14–16). In other words, live your sermons, don't just preach them.

The apostle Peter says without good deeds Jesus' followers will be "ineffective and unproductive" in their knowledge of Jesus Christ (2 Peter 1:5–8). Elsewhere he advises women that if they treat their nonbelieving husbands well, "they [their husbands] may be won

---

* Philip Yancey, "The Holy Inefficiency of Henri Nouwen: A better symbol of the Incarnation, I can hardly imagine," in *Christianity Today,* December 9, 1996.

† Dick Staub, *The Culturally Savvy Christian* (San Francisco: John Wiley & Sons, 2007), 133.

over without words" (1 Peter 3:1, 2). The apostle James goes so far as to say that his actions *are* his witness. "Show me your faith without deeds," he says, almost taunting, "and I will show you my faith by what I do" (James 2:18).

## It's not either/or

Actions may speak louder than words, yet let's not underestimate the importance of words. The most powerful testimony appears when both work together.

Jesus revealed God's love through His words and His life. On one occasion Philip asked, " 'Lord, show us the Father and that will be enough for us.' " Jesus replied, " 'Don't you know me, Philip, even after I have been among you such a long time? Anyone who has seen me has seen the Father. How can you say, "Show us the Father"? ' " (John 14:8, 9). When we see Jesus, we see clearly what God is like.

Jesus revealed a God who identifies with His people and cares for them. As the writer to the Hebrews says, "For we do not have a high priest who is unable to sympathize with our weaknesses, but we have one who has been tempted in every way, just as we are—yet was without sin" (Hebrews 4:15).

Compassion drove everything Jesus said and did. Note how often the Gospel writers say He was "filled with compassion" or "had compassion." Sometimes this meant strongly condemning sin. Jesus often spoke harshly to the religious leaders, but He did it always in love.

Jesus' compassion changed lives. One beautiful example is the leper Jesus healed. He "came back, praising God in a loud voice. He threw himself at Jesus' feet and thanked him" (Luke 17:15, 16). And he was a Samaritan.

People hung on Jesus' words, and "large crowds" traveled with Him (Luke 14:25) and followed Him (Matthew 8:1; 19:2). On one occasion a large crowd pressed against Jesus until He had to get into a boat and teach them from a distance (Matthew 13:2). The Sanhedrin was worried that if they let Him continue, " 'everyone will believe in him' " (John 11:48). Crowds grew so big that the

Pharisees commented, " 'Look how the whole world has gone after him!' " (John 12:19).

Saddened by the death of his good friend and cousin John the Baptist, Jesus at one point withdrew by boat for some private time, presumably to rest and pray. But it wasn't to be. "When Jesus landed and saw a large crowd, he had compassion on them and healed their sick" (Matthew 14:14). Despite His own physical and spiritual needs, Jesus always put the needs of others first.

This Jesus-like compassion inspires the mission of His church today. Mike Ryan, a vice president of the General Conference who stays in touch with the cutting edge of mission, tells the story of Abednego, a Global Mission pioneer. Abednego was working in Sudan—one of the poorest war-ravaged countries in Africa. Abednego went to a training school for Global Mission pioneers. At the end of the meetings he was assigned to start a congregation in a town 287 miles away. Of course, in south Sudan there's virtually no infrastructure. He didn't catch a bus, train, or plane—because there are no buses, trains, or planes. But compelled by the love and compassion Jesus had shown him, Abednego rode his Global Mission bicycle the 287 miles in order to share that love with others.

Arriving there, he found a place to stay and began trying to make friends. The going was hard, and no one showed interest. Then one day, one of the important leaders in the town brought his sick girl to Abednego. "I understand you are a holy man," he said. "I've been to all our healers, and they can do nothing for my girl. Can you please heal her?"

Abednego says that for a moment he didn't know what to do. He said that at the training school they'd taught him how to give Bible studies. They'd taught him how to make contact with people. They'd taught him simple health remedies. There was no training course on how to perform a healing ceremony.

"I can't heal your little girl," Abednego said, looking at the important man. "But I can talk to the Creator of the universe, who can." And so Abednego prayed for the little girl. Over the next few days she regained her full health and strength.

Where Abednego's words had carried little impact, his actions caught attention. Word quickly passed from house to house that a new holy man was in town—a man who knew how to talk to the Creator of the world. Soon Abednego had a group of forty people meeting each Sabbath to worship and praise the Creator. But then the war pressed close and broke up the group as people fled for their lives. Abednego survived the bombing and bullets and fled with the town citizens to hide in the wilderness.

After two months, the occupying army left, and Abednego returned to the city. On the first Sabbath, Abednego was saddened to see only six people attend church. He determined to start again, and after ten months, the number of members had risen to sixty-eight.

One Sabbath, while they were worshiping, two of the missing members returned to worship. Abednego was overjoyed to see them and assured them that the church had been praying for them. He listened to their story. When the bombing came, they fled to a town 140 miles away. They had come back now only to ask Abednego to return with them because they'd prepared twenty-three people for baptism.

"Abednego had been tempted to wonder where God was when he returned to only six members," says Pastor Ryan. "But now he realized that God had bigger plans than he had."

Some time later, another training meeting was held for Global Mission pioneers. Abednego had to ride more than two hundred miles to get there, and on the way a sniper shot him off his bike. He was unharmed but ended up sleeping that night in a ditch.

Abednego finally arrived at the meetings, where Mike met him and heard his story. As the meetings drew to a close, Abednego approached Mike. Something was weighing on his mind. In his worn-out sandals, he looked up and told Mike again how the sniper had shot him off his bike. "Elder Ryan," he said, looking embarrassed, "I'm so sorry, but the bicycle that Global Mission bought me was damaged." Then, looking down at the ground, he added, "I'm sorry to ask, but is there any chance that Global Mission might be willing to buy four new spokes for my bicycle?"

As Mike looked at him, he fought back tears. Four new spokes. A young man who was shot at by snipers, who had to sleep in ditches, who had survived bombs and the strafing of bullets, who rode 287 miles to start a new congregation, and who could talk to the Creator of the universe—*here he was, embarrassed to ask for four new spokes for his bicycle.*

Jesus lived the life of the poor. He was homeless and lived simply. Today the truth He taught is being shared by men and women, boys and girls, who are willing to sacrifice—to share His love through words and action.

## A street musician

My colleague Rick Kajiura and I were visiting Kinshasa, the capital of the Democratic Republic of Congo. Decades of civil war, political corruption, and economic disaster have scarred the people and land. The Adventist Church there is rich in spiritual fervor but poor in finances and resources. Most pastors don't own even a motorbike; they rely on bicycles or public transport instead.

We met Pastor Jeremiah, a former Global Mission pioneer. He wore a well-worn grey suit and played an ancient, battered piano accordion. When he sang, the accordion and his voice blended in an interplay of harmonies. The melody and energy were contagious.

He and his two children walked two hours to attend the Adventist Mission meetings we were holding. His little girl, Josie, and her younger brother, Bennie, joined him in a vocal trio. Josie, in a simple red dress, sang like an angel. Bennie, in his brown trousers and brown shirt—hand-me-downs through several owners—added a major cuteness factor but not a whole lot in the singing department.

We invited them onto the neighborhood street in front of the church so we could film them singing. The dusty street was strewn with litter but alive with activity. As they sang, a crowd soon gathered—attracted by the music and spectacle. The people were smiling, laughing, moving to the music. Pastor Jeremiah was in his element, ministering to the people, and could scarcely contain his enthusiasm.

Jeremiah knows how to sing in church. He enjoys singing for church members. But his passion is getting out into the streets and neighborhoods and sharing with others. Everywhere he goes, his music attracts people and gives him the chance to share the love of Jesus. "I was a professional musician and singing for the devil," he says. "But I met Jesus, and now I want to share my joy with everyone I meet."*

Jesus was a street musician. Sure, He spoke in the synagogues. But His major ministry was on the streets, in homes, in the fields—going to where the people were. And He spoke their language. He mainly told stories, which captured the attention and imagination of the people. His compelling stories carried the ring of truth. As Luke says, "They were amazed at his teaching, because his message had authority" (Luke 4:32). Mark says, "The common people heard Him gladly" (Mark 12:37, NKJV). He portrayed God as a loving Father, sang as a winsome troubadour, and invited people to join God's kingdom, which He said was right at hand.

## The logos

According to Greek philosophers, the *logos* was an all-pervasive life force balancing everything in nature and holding the universe together. Like its modern echoes in the New Age movement, this view was partly correct.

The apostle John gives the *Logos* a name—Jesus, God's Son. Rather than merely maintaining order in the universe, His mission was to restore order by defeating the enemy of darkness.

"In Him was life, and the life was the light of men," John writes. "The light shines in the darkness, and the darkness did not comprehend it" (John 1:4, 5, NKJV).

The *Logos* actually entered the heart of enemy-occupied territory: "the true light that gives light to every man was coming into the world" (verse 9); "The Word became flesh and made his dwelling among us" (verse 14).

---

* To view a video of Pastor Jeremiah and his children singing on the streets of Kinshasa, visit http://www.AdventistMission.org.

God is revealed through Jesus' life and death. Want to see what sin does? See the loving Creator of the universe nailed against the sky on a Roman cross. Want to see what light does? See the loving Creator touch a blind man's eyes, heal a leper, and forgive an adulterous woman.

In some mysterious way on that cross, God Himself took responsibility for dealing with the crazed cancer of sin. He was, to use Ellen White's words, "Himself the victim."* Through His death, He brought life. In His pain, He brought relief. Through the Cross, He bridged the gap that had separated His children from Him. His resurrection—light bursting from the darkness—sealed Lucifer's fate.

Despite losing the war, Lucifer limps on, still enlisting human soldiers on his side and acting as if the conclusion of the great controversy were still in doubt. And in a sense it is. Although God has won the overall war, decisive battles for allegiance are fought daily in each human mind.

Ellen White predicts that as his "crowning act" Lucifer will impersonate Christ and hold the nations enthralled.† It's surprising where we can find modern echoes of her apocalyptic vision. Atheistic philosopher Emile Cioran foresees a "scattered human herd [that] will be united under the guardianship of one pitiless shepherd, a kind of planetary monster before whom the nations will prostrate themselves in an alarm bordering on ecstasy."§

But nobody, especially not the father of lies, can impersonate Jesus. Until that day when he tries, we have been called to seek to emulate the Master, not just in words, but in deeds.

---

* See Ellen White, "The Great Controversy," *Manuscript Releases,* vol. 18, 358–367.

† Ellen White, *The Faith I Live By,* 346.

§ Quoted in Harvey Blume, "Baudy Bandwith," in Sven Birkets, ed., *Tolstoy's Dictaphone: Technology and the Muse* (St. Paul: Graywolf Press, 1996), 256, 257.

# CHAPTER 5

# Jesus: His Kingdom Among Us

A Global Mission pioneer in Kinshasa, the capital of the Democratic Republic of Congo, had been witnessing to a man from another religion. The man accepted most of what he learned about Adventism; his stumbling block was accepting Jesus as more than a prophet.

The young man was an avid reader. He read many books on philosophy and religion—including many of Ellen White's books. Then one day he came to the pioneer and told him he was ready to accept that Jesus was God.

The pioneer was surprised and asked him why. He said that in all his reading, he kept coming across the name of Jesus. It was a name that was influential, widely quoted, and constantly referred to. But he never saw the name of his prophet mentioned anywhere.

Now it's easy to say that his reasoning was flawed; after all, the number of references to Jesus in literature doesn't necessarily prove anything. But for this young man it was enough for him to step over the line into faith.

As far as we know, Jesus wrote no books, painted no pictures, composed no music, but He has inspired wonderful literature, art, and music. Belief in Jesus has transformed lives, abolished slavery, and motivated global humanitarian, medical, and educational work.

Although He was on earth for only a few years, His impact through the centuries has been far greater than that of Plato, Socrates, or any other philosopher.

Today, belief in Jesus is under attack. Various forces undermine the authority of Scripture. Many believe Jesus was a good man, a moral leader, a great teacher, but certainly not the Son of God.

Even within the Christian church, many clergy deny His virgin birth, His miracles, and His resurrection. In 1985, the Westar Institute, a research and educational institute, organized the Jesus Seminar "to renew the quest of the historical Jesus." It now meets twice a year to discuss scholarly papers relating to Jesus. After they debate each agenda item, more than two hundred scholars vote on the authenticity of selected words or acts of Jesus.

We don't need to check the tally or the polls. Christians study and live by Jesus and His teachings as recorded in the New Testament because we know they tell us the truth about ourselves, and they change our lives. In these pages we meet a unique Person—the holy Son of God, who was constantly criticized for spending time with "bad people." People, perhaps, such as you and me.

## Life lessons

Jesus' friend and disciple the apostle John wrote one of the first books about Him. Tens of thousands have been written since. John concludes his book, "Jesus did many other things as well. If every one of them were written down, I suppose that even the whole world would not have room for the books that would be written" (John 21:25).

Born in the town of Bethlehem, Jesus grew up in Nazareth, where He worked in Joseph's carpenter shop. A strictly observant Jew, He followed the Law of Moses and participated in Jewish services and rituals.

In the sense of formal schooling, He wasn't highly educated. On one occasion He spoke at the temple. People looking on "were amazed and asked, 'How did this man get such learning without having studied?' " (John 7:15). Jesus related to people from all walks of life.

"Jesus increased in wisdom and stature," writes Luke, "and in favour with God and man" (Luke 2:52, KJV). He lived to the age of thirty-three and spent only three and a half years out of the carpenter's shop. But, as John says, He did so much in so little time. During those action-packed years, He traveled through Palestine, teaching a radical way of understanding God and the world.

Jesus spoke constantly about God's love and the way we should live. More important, He *demonstrated* God's love and *showed* how to live. He healed the sick, helped hopeless people find God, and lifted stains of guilt from the guilty. Not everyone, particularly the religious leaders, was pleased. His teachings and ministry eventually led to His death. As John says, "Having loved his own who were in the world, he now showed them the full extent of his love" (John 13:1). He adds, "This is how we know what love is: Jesus Christ laid down his life for us" (1 John 3:16).

How did Jesus affect people? His disciple Peter exclaimed, " 'You are the Messiah, the Son of the living God' " (Matthew 16:16, NLT). The common people loved Him. Even the temple guards confessed, " 'We have never heard anyone speak like this!' " (John 7:46, NLT).

Jesus downplayed His popularity. In fact, when He did something spectacular, He usually told people to keep quiet about it. Though He shunned the spotlight (John 7:3), crowds constantly followed Him.

Wealth didn't make Jesus special. In fact, He was poor, even homeless. He never charged for His work and never tried to raise funds. Money was never important to Him. As He once said, you can't serve God and money at the same time (Matthew 6:24). He added, " 'And don't be concerned about what to eat and what to drink. Don't worry about such things' " (Luke 12:29, NLT).

Power didn't make Jesus special. Of course, He had all power in heaven and earth (Matthew 28), but it was a selfless power. He healed diseases, restored broken lives, and left pious hypocrites speechless.

The apostle John identifies what made Jesus' ministry special: "The one who existed from the beginning, whom we have heard and seen. We saw him with our own eyes and touched him with our own hands. He is the Word of life" (1 John 1:1, NLT).

The unique thing about Jesus is that He is God in human form: "And the Word was made flesh, and dwelt among us" (John 1:14, KJV). And what was He like? Jesus was "full of unfailing love and faithfulness" (John 1:14, NLT).

## Amplified distortions

When Jesus sent out His disciples for ministry, He gave them important principles for sharing the gospel with those in different cultures, with differing backgrounds, in different environments. His principles are just as crucial today as they were two thousand years ago.

Dr. Jerald Whitehouse, director of the Global Center for Adventist Muslim Relations, operated by Global Mission, tells of living on a mission compound some years ago. Followers of another religion held services in a building nearby. They attached loudspeakers to their building, and each day sent an amplified message toward the Adventist compound.

The message was in the local language, which Jerald didn't understand. He asked the local people on the Adventist compound to translate, but none could understand it either because the message was terribly distorted through the speakers. Those delivering the message knew what they wanted to say and, no doubt, said it. But it had absolutely no effect on their listeners except to disturb their peace.

Are we sometimes like those trying to send a message through speakers? What can we do to make sure we don't distort our message in the delivery?

Charles Kraft was a missionary in a remote area of northeast Nigeria. He says that after church meetings people would ask, "Why does the Christian God not respect our old men?" He learned that the older male leaders of the village felt that any meeting where they weren't invited to speak first insulted them and the village.

He also discovered other messages that he didn't know were being communicated:

South England Conference

# Adventist Muslim Relations Retreat
## 29 April – 1 May 2011

*'NETWORKING FOR MUSLIM OUTREACH'*

Wokefield Park, Goodboys Lane, Mortimer, Reading,
Berks RG7 3AE

*We would like to Welcome you all to this AMR Retreat 2011 at Woke-field Park. We welcome Pastor Oscar Osindo, GC AMR Associate. We extend a warm welcome to Pastor Don McFarlane, BUC President and Pastor Michael Simpson, NEC Church Growth Director.*
*We trust that you will find this year's AMR Retreat helpful, informative and that it will enrich your experience as you seek to reach your Muslim friends and neighbours.*

*Pastor Petras Bahadur*
*AMR Director*

# Friday

*Co-ordinator: Mr A Lethbridge*

| | | |
|---|---|---|
| 15:00 - 18:00 | Arrival & Registration | |
| 18:30 - 19:30 | **Supper** | |
| 19:30 - 19:40 | Worship in Songs | Ms L Byng |
| 19:40 - 19:55 | Worship | Angaza children |
| 19:55 - 20:05 | Welcome and Introductions | Pastor P Bahadur |
| 20:05 - 20:25 | Opening Address | Pastor D McFarlane BUC President |
| 20:25 - 21:15 | Session I | Pastor O Osindo |
| 21:15 - 21:30 | Interactive Workshops | |

Best of all, we can co-operate with God Himself in reaching the individual goal He has set for us and in helping others to fulfil His plan for them. Let us then examine this claim for ourselves and not rest until we have found the answer.

Paul (writing of the Old Testament) says, *"All Scripture is given by inspiration of God.....2 Timothy 3:16* Peter's words corroborate this. *"For the prophecy came not in old time by the will of man: but holy men of God spake as they were moved by the Holy Ghost."*
*2 Peter 1:21*

Had the entire Bible been written by one man or by two or more in collaboration, one might reasonably doubt the validity of the claim to divine authorship, but these men are not here claiming divine authority for their own writings but for those of men whom they had never seen, men who lived and died centuries before.

Even more striking than this, is the complete harmony of doctrine revealed in the Bible. The men who wrote it were not only separated by time. They varied greatly in education, in their occupations, and in their experience and social position. They wrote in at least three different languages and in many varied styles, yet their writings all combine to form one united book and bear the stamp of one mastermind.

## 2. What part does prophecy play in the Bible?

God Himself has chosen prophecy as the greatest proof of His infinite superiority over all other beings.

> *"Remember the former things of old: for I am God, and there is none else; I am God, and there is none like me. Declaring the end from the beginning, and from ancient times the things that hare not yet done, saying, My counsel shall stand, and I will do all my pleasure:"* Isaiah 46:9,10 (See also 42:9.)

A shrewd man, reasoning from cause to effect, may sometimes forecast the near future with some accuracy, but what mere human being can predict the future centuries ahead with strict precision? The Bible contains many such predictions, written by men who themselves did not fully comprehend the import and extent of the prophecies they made, thus pointing to a source outside of, and higher than, themselves.

### 3. What effect does the Bible have on lives?

One of the most convincing proofs of its divine origin is the effect of the Bible on those who read it. No other book has the power to transform debased sinners into saints, and cannibals into kind-hearted men. The reading of the Bible replaces ignorance with knowledge, folly with wisdom, fear with courage, and hate with love. Wherever the Bible goes, churches, schools, and hospitals spring up, cleanliness takes the place of filth, and barbarous practices are outlawed. Its influence is invariably includes the ennobling and uplifting.

### 4. Does science contradict the Word of God?

Further evidence of the truth of the Bible is its complete accord with all the known facts of science. Since truth cannot contradict itself, we should naturally expect the Word of God to be in harmony with observable scientific knowledge. And so it is. Contrary to popular belief, no discovery ever has been made that disproves the teachings of the Scriptures. Any apparent difference between them is the result of human theorising on these two great sources of knowledge. One great writer has said, *"Human knowledge of both material and spiritual things is partial and imperfect; therefore many are unable to harmonise their views of science with Scripture statement. Many accept mere theories and speculations as scientific facts, and think that God's Word is to be tested by the teachings of 'science falsely so called.'"*

### 5. In what way was it preserved?

Added to its claim to divine inspiration is the Bible assertion that it has been providentially preserved from adulteration and loss. In *Psalm 12:6, 7* we read, *"The words of the Lord are pure words: as silver tried in a furnace of earth, purified seven times. Thou shalt keep them, O Lord, thou shalt preserve them from this generation for ever."*

As we read the story of how the Bible has come down to us through the centuries before the art of printing, we cannot but be impressed by the marvellous way in which its accuracy has been maintained. Despite the fact that it has been copied and re-copied times out of number by thousands of different hands and in many different languages, the variations that occur in the thousands of manuscripts that have come down to us are so slight as to make not even a shadow of change in the teaching and significance of the sacred Scriptures.

## 6. Will the Bible be overthrown?

The Bible has triumphantly withstood every effort of man to overthrow it. It has been suppressed and withheld from the common people, whole editions of it have been gathered together and burned, and innumerable books have been written to refute it. No other book has ever been subjected to such continuous and determined opposition, but still it stands, immovable and unconquerable. As one great Christian leader said, *"The Bible is an anvil that has worn out many hammers. Truly, the Word of our God shall stand for ever."*

## 7. Why was the Bible written?

Without the Word of God we should know nothing of how the human race originated, of the great and marvellous plan of salvation, or of the promised triumphant victory of right over wrong and the final extermination of every trace of sin and evil. True, we should not be entirely without a knowledge of God, for all nature proclaims His being and His ways. *"The heavens declare the glory of God; and the firmament sheweth his handywork." Psalm 19:1*

> *"For the invisible things of him from the creation of the world*
> *are clearly seen, being understood by the things that are made,*
> *even his eternal power and God head; so that they are without*
> *excuse: God's invisible qualities - His eternal power and divine*
> *nature have been clearly seen, being understood from what has*
> *been made, so that men are without excuse." Romans 1:20*

But nature in itself is not sufficient. In their pride and self-sufficiency, men have attempted to interpret natural phenomena by their own unaided wisdom and have reached unwarranted and un-provable conclusions. God saw that we should need a special revelation as a safeguard against false theories about Him and His works. The chief purpose of the Bible is to make known to fallen men and women the way of salvation through Jesus Christ.

The Old and New Testaments combine to uplift Him as the one and only Saviour, *"That was the true Light, which lighteth every man that cometh into the world.." John 1:9* .

> *"But these are written that ye might believe that Jesus is the*
> *Christ, the Son of God; and that believing ye might have life*
> *through his name." John 20:31 .(See 2 Timothy 3:15).*

5

In pages of this Book, we find the divine definitions of right and wrong, man's duty to God and to his fellow-men, and all the doctrine necessary for his enlightenment. Says Paul, *"All Scripture is given by inspiration of God, and is profitable for doctrine, for reproof for correction for instruction in righteousness:"* 2 Timothy 3:16, 17.

Finally, the Bible has been given to man that he might know, in broad outline, what the future holds, and be prepared for the coming of Christ.

> *"We have also a more sure word of prophecy; whereunto ye do well that ye take heed, as unto a light that shineth in a dark place, until the day dawn, and the day star arise in your hearts:"* 2 Peter 1:19

## 8. What are the conditions to be met?

The Bible is a big book, and many interpretations have been put upon it. Can we be sure of gaining a correct understanding of its teachings? Are there any rules to be followed? Is there an unerring guide?

The answer to all these questions is, **Yes**. The God who gave us the Bible and who has so miraculously preserved it for us has also promised us wisdom to understand it and has given us instructions how to obtain it. We may have felt that those who are well educated have a great advantage over the less learned. How much easier it would be, we have thought, if the Bible were set out like a school textbook. Then we should know exactly what it meant.

"God is no respecter of persons." A saving knowledge of His Word does not depend on a high degree of intelligence or an advanced education, though these things are not to be despised. Addressing His Father, Jesus said, on one occasion, *"....I thank thee, O Father, Lord of heaven and earth, because thou hast hid these things from the wise and prudent, and hast revealed them unto babes."* Matthew 11:25 .

If we would understand the Scriptures, we must become teachable as little children.

There are three other great essential conditions to be met.

*The first is a deep and persevering desire to know the truth for ourselves.

# Sabbath

*Co-ordinator: Mr E Shelufumo*

| | | |
|---|---|---|
| 07:30 - 08:45 | **Breakfast** | |
| 08:45 - 09:00 | Worship in Songs | Ms S Delliston |
| 09:00 - 09:15 | Devotional | Mr E Ramharacksingh<br>SEC Treasurer |
| 09:15 - 10:00 | SEC Ministry Highlights | Pastor P Bahadur |
| 10:00 - 10:45 | Experience of AMR | |
| 10:45 - 11:00 | **Q & A** | |
| 11:00 - 11:15 | **Break** | |
| 11:15 - 12:45 | Session II | Pastor O Osindo |
| 12:45 - 13:00 | **Q & A** | |
| 13:00 - 14:00 | **Lunch** | |
| 14:00 - 16:00 | Free time | |
| 16:00 - 16:45 | Interactive Discussion (split in groups) | |
| 16:45 - 17:30 | Session III | Pastor O Osindo |
| 17:30 - 17:45 | **Worship** | Ms L Byng |
| 17:45 - 18:30₄₅ | Experiences & Testimonies | Mr A Lethbridge |
| 18:30 - 19:30 | **Supper** | |
| 19:30 | Free time | |

# Sunday

| | | |
|---|---|---|
| 07:30 - 09:00 | **Breakfast** (and preparations for vacating your room) | |
| 09:00 - 09:15 | Worship | NEC |
| 09:15 - 09:30 | Devotional | Pastor M Simpson<br>NEC Ch.Growth Director |
| 09:30 - 10:30 | Practical suggestions<br>for reaching Muslims | Pastor P Bahadur |
| 10:30 –10:45 | **Break** | |
| 10:45  -11:30 | Session IIII | Pastor O Osindo |
| 11:30 - 12:30 | Planning & Feedback<br>SEC/NEC | Pastor P Bahadur<br>& Pastor M Simpson |
| 12:30 - 13:00 | Commitment & Closing Remarks | Pastor P Bahadur |
| 13:00 - 14:00 | **Lunch** | |
| 14:00 | Departure | |

On Sunday rooms need to be vacated by 10am.
We would appreciate your full co-operation with this.
If you need to store your luggage until the closing of the programme you can find
the storage room next to reception.

1. The playing of Western hymns implied that God accepted Western music but not their traditional music.
2. Sermons on intellectual topics (rather than practical, pictorial-type sermons) gave the impression that only Western-educated people who "think like White people" could understand the messages. By implication, only they could be acceptable to God.
3. Speaking about a God who did wonderful things in the past, but apparently can't still do them, provided them with little reason for following Jesus.

Kraft concluded that the people therefore found "the primary attraction of Christianity to be in the things offered by Western culture, not in the things spoken of in the Bible."* The message he was trying to share got distorted through his loudspeakers.

Jesus taught the disciples vital principles for clearly communicating the good news of the kingdom. His followers were an unconventional mix: fishermen, religious leaders, Roman centurions, lepers, prostitutes, business people, and tax collectors. Luke says, "Tax collectors and other notorious sinners often came to listen to Jesus teach" (Luke 15:1, NLT). From this group Jesus chose His twelve disciples, ordinary men you and I probably wouldn't have voted as "The Twelve Most Likely to Succeed." We would have looked for more qualified candidates. But, of course, God has a history of choosing people we wouldn't choose.

Most were young and from different backgrounds. They ranged from Matthew the tax-gatherer—whom other Jews hated—to Simon the Zealot, a hero for fighting to free the people from the Romans. William Barclay says if Simon the Zealot had met Matthew the tax-gatherer anywhere other than in the company of Jesus, he would have stuck a dagger in him.

Jesus had been touring Galilee, where He was preaching, teaching, and healing. Though exhausted, He was still concerned for the

---

* Charles H. Kraft, *Culture, Communication, and Christianity* (William Carey Library, 2001), 378.

crowds who demanded so much of Him. As Jesus looked, He had "compassion on them, because they were harassed and helpless, like sheep without a shepherd" (Matthew 9:36).

Jesus knew the people's needs; He'd seen them firsthand. It was now time to send out His first class—the twelve disciples—to meet that need.

In Jesus we see the principles on which the universe is founded. We find in Jesus how human beings should act. The disciples had been with Jesus only a year or so. But they'd walked and talked with the One who is the Way, the Truth, and the Life. The time had come to put their learning into practice. Before sending them out, Jesus gave some last-minute advice, recorded in Matthew 10.

Let's look at the principles Jesus taught them:

**The kingdom of heaven is at hand.** Jesus told His class to proclaim that the kingdom of heaven is at hand (Matthew 10:7). It wasn't going to arrive when the Romans were overthrown. The kingdom of heaven was now. *Now* people were able to see Jesus. *Now* they were able to emulate the way He lived. *Now* they could see how the kingdom operated in real life. *Now* they could become part of that kingdom.

Today many factors work to separate spirituality from real life. Professor Stephen Carter writes, "The message of contemporary culture seems to be that it is perfectly all right to *believe* that stuff— we have freedom of conscience, folks can believe what they like— but you really ought to keep it to yourself, especially if your beliefs are the sort that cause you to act in ways that are . . . well . . . a bit unorthodox."*

Religion is seen as "otherworldly," as something that doesn't have anything to do with day-to-day living. It's what you may choose to do on Sunday morning. Religion refers to an afterlife but makes no difference to our real lives—the world of raising kids, school, shopping, eating, sexuality, work, recreation.

---

* Stephen L. Carter, *The Culture of Disbelief: How American Law and Politics Trivialize Religious Devotion* (New York: BasicBooks, 1993), 25.

But Jesus was talking about far more than just "pie in the sky." He was talking about God's kingdom being present *now*, shaping and influencing every facet of our lives. Separating the spiritual and the physical is an ancient heresy, which Gnostics promoted. Their esoteric, inward-focused views threatened to distort the teachings of the early Christian church. True Christianity infiltrates and influences all aspects of life, the spiritual and the physical. Jesus compared the kingdom of heaven to yeast, which doesn't stay separate. It affects the whole lump of dough; it permeates the entire loaf of bread.

**Be wise and harmless.** Jesus told His class they needed to be wise. Rather than saying something predictable such as "be as wise as Solomon," He used shocking imagery. He told them to be as "wise as serpents." When Jews thought of a serpent, they remembered the Genesis story of the cunning snake in the Garden of Eden. But there was an infinite difference between that serpent and what Jesus wanted them to be. They were to be as wise as snakes but also as "harmless as doves" (Matthew 10:16, KJV).

Jesus demonstrated this principle in His choice of twelve men as His disciples. It seems unfair today that Jesus didn't include any women. But as much as Jesus might have wanted to include women among the Twelve, He knew what would happen if He did. It wouldn't have been tolerated. No Jewish male would have listened to a woman teach, and rumors would have spread about the group. Women did travel with Jesus and His disciples at times and actually kept them financially afloat. "After this, Jesus traveled about from one town and village to another, proclaiming the good news of the kingdom of God. The Twelve were with him, and also some women who had been cured of evil spirits and diseases: Mary (called Magdalene) from whom seven demons had come out; Joanna the wife of Cuza, the manager of Herod's household; Susanna; and many others. These women were helping to support them out of their own means" (Luke 8:1–3).

Jesus didn't merely support the status quo. He treated women as equals to men. He gave them a dignity and a status they'd never experienced. Women loved Him so much they followed Him wherever He went. He spoke openly with them. Women were important to Him. As with other issues, Jesus wisely addressed the inclusion of women. He wasn't willing to go too far against people's cultural expectations and thereby jeopardize His cause. As it was, He ultimately was killed for going against the expectations of those He'd come to save.

Wherever we go, we find cultural expectations—from wearing a coat when you preach to not crossing your legs at worship services. Some norms may seem wonderful; some may seem misguided, incorrect, ridiculous. But they exist, they're real, and we can't afford to ignore them. Jesus would have us, like His class, be as wise as serpents and as harmless as doves. We need to be sensitive to the people we're trying to reach.

Jesus also told His class to go to the Israelites, not to the Gentiles (Matthew 10:5, 6). Again, at first glance, this seems unfair. Why should one group get special treatment?

Jesus knew that if His disciples went first to the Gentiles, they'd lose most of the Jewish people He was trying to reach. Jesus also knew the bigoted attitudes of His disciples. Yes, they'd sat at His feet. Yes, they'd heard the good news of the kingdom. But, like us, they weren't perfect. It would take time for them to understand the full implications of the kingdom—which included Gentiles.

The attitudes and understandings of those receiving and delivering the good news were less than ideal. But Jesus knew we have to work the best we can within the circumstances we have. We work within the way things are, just as Jesus did.

No matter where we go, we'll encounter people who see things differently. We can stand up and strongly proclaim our points of view and, as a result, immediately alienate people. Or we can follow Jesus' advice and recognizing a time for restraint. We must remember that not everyone comes from our background or has gone through our experience. Not everyone holds the same interests.

Jesus encourages us to show love and tolerance. Be willing to learn. Show sensitivity. Be as wise as serpents. Once we've earned people's trust and friendship, we can share more fully. In fact, it's the only way we'll ever be able to break down barriers—inside or out of the church. It's the only way we can be as harmless as doves.

**Minister holistically.** Jesus' commission to His disciples wasn't limited to teaching and preaching. Certainly, the disciples were called to prepare people for the kingdom of heaven. But in an important sense, the kingdom was already with them. That meant they should show concern for people's physical, emotional, and social needs. They were to heal, as well as preach (Matthew 10:8).

## Living in reality

British writer Malcolm Muggeridge describes an imaginary scenario involving a Roman media tycoon named Lucius Gradus the Elder. This tycoon discovers Jesus and immediately recognizes His potential. Jesus could become a media icon, even a superstar. All Lucius has to do is take Jesus to Rome, put Him on TV, and watch Him reach the masses—not just a few scruffy hangers-on in Galilee.

Muggeridge imagined this as a possible fourth temptation of Christ—which, like the others, Jesus would have resisted. "He was concerned with truth and reality," says Muggeridge, whereas the tycoon was concerned with "fantasy and images."*

Today images saturate our world. More than ever we need the reality taught and modeled by Jesus. The writer to the Hebrews says, "For the word of God is living and active. Sharper than any double-edged sword, it penetrates even to dividing soul and spirit, joints and marrow; it judges the thoughts and attitudes of the heart" (Hebrews 4:12).

The apostle John said Jesus "knew what was in a man" (John 2:25). He knows our motivations, speaks truth to us, and remains the only infallible Guide in this world and the next. Jesus wasn't selling some shiny product that would wear out and have to be replaced. He was giving truth. He was offering something unique

---

* Malcolm Muggeridge, *Christ and the Media* (Regent College Publishing, 2003), 41–43. (Originally published in 1976.)

and that ultimately was satisfying. And it's still a free offer—
" 'Whoever drinks the water that I give him will never thirst' " (John 4:14).

It must have annoyed someone as pragmatic as Judas. Can't you hear him wheedling Jesus to refuse to talk to groups of under a thousand people? "Lord, the way You try to win people is to . . . to . . . I don't know how to say it, but You have to get real. If You let me organize it, we can reach many more people. Look, I've got this friend named Lucius Gradus . . ."

Jesus said No to framing fantasies and to packaging images. The foundation of His ministry was personal contact. Within decades His message had spread through the then-known world. It would have shocked Gradus. But it happened for one reason, and that was because people had been touched by the Master's hand.

And by His imperfect disciples too.

# CHAPTER 6

# Jesus: No Hammers, Please

The story is told of ten-year-old Johnny who came home from Sunday School, and his mother asked him what he'd learned.

"Well," he replied, "our teacher told us about when God sent Moses behind enemy lines to rescue the Israelites from the Egyptians. When they came to the Red Sea, Moses called for the engineers to build a pontoon bridge. After they'd all crossed over, they looked back and saw the Egyptian tanks coming. Quick as a flash, Moses got out his iPhone and e-mailed headquarters to send bombers in order to blow up the bridge and save the Israelites."

"Johnny!" exclaimed his mother. "Is that really the way your teacher told that story?"

"Well, not exactly," he said. "But if I told it her way, you'd never believe it."

Without knowing it, Johnny had stumbled on the vital mission principle of *contextualization*—communicating spiritual truths in the most effective way possible. He may have abused the principle, but at least he was trying.

How do we communicate the hope we find in Jesus in ways that are accessible and relevant? How do we communicate in postmodern societies, where many people no longer believe in God or in the Bible? How do we share in societies dominated by one of the other major world religions that have radically different spiritual world-views than ours?

Let's look again at the teachings and example of Jesus, the Master Missionary.

## Knocking on doors

The apostle John pictures Jesus knocking at a door saying, " 'Here I am! I stand at the door and knock. If anyone hears my voice and opens the door, I will come in and eat with him, and he with me' " (Revelation 3:20). Jesus doesn't stand at the door with a battering ram. He doesn't even try to open the door with a master key. He knocks, waits respectfully, and leaves the choice to us whether or not we open the door.

God invites us to salvation. He doesn't try to trick, cajole, bribe, or force. The finale of the book of Revelation beautifully describes a God who invites: "And the Spirit and the bride say, Come. And let him that heareth say, Come. And let him that is athirst come. And whosoever will, let him take the water of life freely" (Revelation 22:17, KJV).

The water of life is free to "whosoever will." Too often we get the idea that it's our task to "convert" people, rather than leaving it to the Holy Spirit. And so we try different methods to open the doors of people's hearts. We talk about "entering wedges," a wonderful metaphor if we're talking about attractive ways to open the way for people to accept Jesus. It's not so appealing if we mean slipping these wedges between the door and the doorframe, grabbing a hammer, and forcing open the door.

Our calling is to join Jesus in knocking on doors, inviting people to open their lives to Him. Our calling is to pray that the Holy Spirit will touch the emotions and intellects of people to open up to His love. Jesus Himself was so interested in opening doors to people that He said, "I am the door" (John 10:7, KJV).

That's why we need to be careful when some enthusiastic evangelists, motivated by good intentions, talk about "closing the sale" to "gain decisions." Or when we read about a "sure-proof, five-step method" of witnessing. There are no "sure-proof" methods. A decision to follow Jesus isn't a product to be bought or sold. Jesus knocks on doors, but He doesn't need to employ the techniques of a "pr-eowned-car" salesperson. That wonderful moment when a human being exercises the gift of free choice to open the door to God can't be reduced to a mere business transaction.

Simon the sorcerer saw Peter and John lay their hands on people in order to bestow the Holy Spirit on them. He was so impressed that he offered to pay them for the power to do the same thing. " 'May your money perish with you, because you thought you could buy the gift of God with money!' " Peter roared. " 'You have no part or share in this ministry, because your heart is not right before God' " (Acts 8:20, 21).

In its February 2007 issue, *Travel & Leisure* magazine ran an article about Mongolia entitled "Inland Empire," in which an elder in another denomination was quoted as saying that Seventh-day Adventists bribe Mongolians to convert. I wrote to the editor: "Adventist leadership in the country has checked with all church employees and found no evidence of such a practice. First, the Adventist Church and its members in Mongolia aren't exactly flush with cash to go around bribing people. But more important, it goes against our freedom-loving principles. We prefer the old-fashioned method of respecting people's free choice, and trusting entirely to the attractiveness of the Christian message. We are grateful that it has brought our church success in more than two hundred countries of the world you celebrate so well in your magazine."

Of all the gifts God has given human beings, perhaps the most powerful is free choice. He respects people's right to exercise it. So should we.

## Sneaking in truth

Flannery O'Connor, the famous writer from America's South, tried to share her Christian faith through stories. "I have found from reading my own writing," she said, "that my subject in fiction is the action of grace in territory held by the devil." Some have criticized her for using shocking images and characters. She responded that because most of her audience didn't share her beliefs, she needed to startle them. "When you can assume that your audience holds the same beliefs you do," she said, "you can relax a little and use more normal means of talking to it; when you have to assume that it does not, then you have to make your vision apparent by shock—to the hard of hearing you shout, and for the almost-blind you draw large and startling figures."*

Doris Betts, a later writer, also from the South, writes, "That is certainly one method, but I—like many mothers and kindergarten teachers—have found that the whisper can also be effective . . . there's a range between times when Jesus inveighed strongly against a 'generation of vipers' and other times when He might stoop and silently scratch words in the ground. At times Jesus pronounced His woes against the religious leaders. But at other times He told parables that sneaked the truth in through the back door, and gently knocked on the hearts of his audience."†

Of course, parables can hit audiences squarely in the head too. On one occasion God used a parable to knock sense into the man He had chosen to occupy the throne of Israel. If committing adultery with Bathsheba hadn't been horrible enough, King David added the sin of murdering her husband, Uriah. We might expect this from a backstreet thug or mafia kingpin, but not someone God called a man after His own heart. In breathtaking understatement, the writer of 2 Samuel says God was "displeased" (2 Samuel 11:27).

Immediately God sent His prophet Nathan to David. But rather than condemning David for his heinous sin, Nathan told him a parable, a single story that slipped truth in the back door. The story caught David's attention and sympathies and threw him right off the scent of what Nathan was getting at.

Two men—one rich, the other poor—lived in a town. While the rich man owned many sheep and cattle, the poor man owned only a little lamb that he'd worked hard to buy. The lamb grew up with

---

* Flannery O'Connor, quoted in Dick Staub, *The Culturally Savvy Christian* (San Francisco: John Wiley & Sons, 2007), 193.

† Doris Betts, "Whispering Hope," in *Image: A Journal of the Arts & Religion*, issue 7, Fall 1994.

his children, ate from his own plate, drank from his own cup. He cuddled the little lamb as if it were his own daughter.

One day a guest visited the rich man's house. Instead of killing one of his own sheep for dinner, the rich man seized the poor man's beloved lamb, butchered it, and served it to the guest.

In telling this story, Nathan was an expert fisherman. He hooked David's attention then slowly started reeling him in. As Nathan finished the story, David exclaimed, " 'As surely as the Lord lives, . . . any man who would do such a thing deserves to die!' " (2 Samuel 12:5, NLT).

Having hooked his fish, Nathan now landed him: "Thou art the man," he exclaimed (verse 7, KJV).

Such is the power of a parable. It engages our heart, grabs our attention, and smacks us with truth when we least expect it. No wonder it was Jesus' main method of teaching.

Jesus layered His parables with meaning. Two people could hear the same story and, depending on where they were spiritually, receive different messages. A straight delivery could deliver too much information or raise such an obvious barrier that people wouldn't listen.

Mark 4 contains four of Jesus' parables: the farmer sowing seed, the lamp, the growing seed, and the mustard seed. At the end of the final parable, Mark explains, "With many similar parables Jesus spoke the word to them, as much as they could understand" (Mark 4:33).

When spiritually training my two-year-old daughter, Bethany, I don't try to teach much more than "Jesus loves me, this I know." Trying to explain intricacies of the history of Christology or principles of prophetic interpretation would be a waste. In the same way, through parables Jesus measured out truth like medicine; He gave hearers just the right dose for their spiritual needs.

In our witness we must avoid giving people living water from a fire hose. Following Jesus' example means looking for ways to reach people from novel angles, perhaps when they least expect it. It means shaping our message to our audience, matching their interest and levels of understanding.

## The touch of the Master's hand

" 'Come to me, all you who are weary and burdened, and I will give you rest,' " said Jesus. " 'Take my yoke upon you and learn from me, for I am gentle and humble in heart, and you will find rest for your souls. For my yoke is easy and my burden is light' " (Matthew 11:28–30). He opened His arms to all, especially those rejected or looked-down on by "good" religious people.

Jesus attracted sinners. They invited him to their parties. They enjoyed spending time with Him. Jesus actually earned a reputation as a party-goer and was criticized for "hanging out" with sinful people. He became known as "friend of . . . sinners" (Matthew 11:19), a wonderful nickname. On one occasion the Pharisees saw Jesus eating with tax collectors and "sinners" at Matthew's house. They asked His disciples why He ate with such people. Jesus heard what they said and replied, " 'It is not the healthy who need a doctor, but the sick. But go and learn what this means: "I desire mercy, not sacrifice." For I have not come to call the righteous, but sinners' " (Matthew 9:10–13).

Have you noticed something about "righteous" people within the church who are quick to stand up and condemn, call sin by its right name, and refuse to compromise standards in any way? Who throw chapter and verse at young people, decry the sins of the church community, and never manage to smile? They don't attract sinners. Sinners don't cling to them. And they don't lead people to Jesus.

My friend James Coffin is senior pastor of the Markham Woods Seventh-day Adventist Church in Orlando, Florida. Their Statement of Philosophy says, "Our church family is not a fraternity for the perfect but a support group for those needing growth. Our goal is to accept people where they are on their spiritual journey, providing an environment where less-than-perfect people can be confident of love, acceptance and forgiveness in a spiritual family."

This congregation hopes that the prophet Isaiah's description of the coming Messiah (Isaiah 42:2, 3) could apply to Markham Woods: "He will not shout or cry out, or raise his voice in the streets. A bruised reed he will not break, and a smoldering wick he will not snuff out."

# Jesus: No Hammers, Please

Jesus knew the power of the personal touch of love. He mingled with people from all walks of life. His feet got covered in sand, His hands got dirty. He wore human skin, breathed air, walked our earth. He wasn't content to sit in heaven, flick a switch, and miraculously send us hope long-distance. Salvation wasn't accomplished via celestial remote control. Jesus personally brought hope.

In a public hospital in Arua, Uganda, a young mother-to-be awaited the birth of her first baby. She'd had a long, hard labor. Lying on her hospital bed, she could only whisper with the contractions, "God will help." Nearby stood Adventist missionary Kristina Muelhauser, patting her arm and encouraging her. Then they took the mother-to-be away for a C-section.

Kristina lives in Arua with her husband, Darrel, and their youngest child, Harmony. Darrel directs ministerial training for the Adventist Church in nearby south Sudan. Kristina homeschools Harmony and helps as a midwife in the local community.

In the evening, she returned to the hospital to see the baby. There she was, a chubby girl. The family, all Muslims, surrounded the beaming young mother.

The next morning Kristina returned to check on the mother and discovered the baby had died during the night. "The mother lay still in the bed with her eyes closed, shutting out the other forty women and their babies who were in the same room with her," says Kristina. "My heart felt like lead."

Kristina rushed home and found a soft little white hat with yellow tulips that she had knitted many years before. She tucked the little hat in her bag and rode her bike back to the hospital. The baby's grandmother stood sadly at the end of her daughter's bed. She spoke no English.

Kristina told the nurse the hat was for the baby. The nurse was surprised but explained to the grandmother what Kristina wanted to do. Student nurses and women in other beds quietly watched.

"The African Muslim women here cover their heads, but not their faces," says Kristina. "I could easily see the tears flow down the black cheeks of the dear grandmother as she uncovered the baby's head. Together, Muslim and Christian, Black and White, we put the little hat on, our hands and hearts touching.

"The mother had not moved or opened her eyes through all of this," Kristina adds. "She lay still in the bed, silent in her grief and pain. I asked the grandma to bring the baby for the mother to see her one last time. The mother opened her eyes. Tenderly I patted the round little cheek of the baby, and then the mother, as we all wept quietly together."

Kristina says she and her family are ordinary. She never had any great desire for overseas mission service. She didn't want to leave their family and cozy home in northern Maine, in the United States. But all that has changed. She's found meaning and purpose in following the example of the Savior, who modeled this type of selfless love.*

## Spiritual gifts and gaffes

To help the church share the good news, God has equipped us with a variety of spiritual gifts. Not all are preachers. Not all are teachers. Not all are public evangelists. Not all can go door to door. But each of us has been given gifts that can help communicate hope in Jesus.

When I was a child, I learned the violin. As you know, the violin is a four-stringed instrument that can make beautiful music. Despite years of lessons, I never discovered how to make mine do that.

The problem is that there are so many variables when playing the violin—fingers have to be on the exact part of the string, bow in correct position, vibrato correct. When all this is handled with skill, the result is melodic. When it's not, the noise can kill another human at twenty paces. It sounds like an operatic soprano with laryngitis being strangled under water.

At home I was diligently practicing my scales and arpeggios when my brother, Wayne, yelled out, "You won't be taking that thing to heaven!"

---

* To read more stories about the Muelhausers and other missionary families, visit the blogs at http://www.AdventistMission.org.

"Why not?" I replied, foolishly setting myself up.

"The Bible says there'll be no vile thing there," he pronounced gleefully.

My mother is gifted musically (and in many other ways). She plays the piano and organ and has a beautiful voice. She encouraged me to play special features at church. Only a loving mother could do it. I'd get up and be so nervous that my bow would bounce on the strings as if it were a trampoline. The fingers on the strings would dance an amazingly aggressive vibrato out of sheer terror.

I eventually realized that public performance on the violin wasn't my gift. I wasn't a concert violinist, and I didn't have to be.

If you can't sing, don't join the choir. If you're not a preacher, don't preach. And if you can't play the violin, please, please, don't play the violin. Find your gifts and, with God's grace—*use them.*

The apostle James writes, "But someone will say, 'You have faith; I have deeds.' Show me your faith without deeds, and I will show you my faith by what I do" (James 2:18).

We can talk about faith, and we should. We can talk about doctrines, and we should. We can talk about hope in Jesus, and we should. But the most effective and convincing way to communicate the love of Jesus is to show people the practical difference it makes in our individual lives and can make in theirs.

This is something that speaks to all languages and cuts across all cultures.

# CHAPTER 7

# John: Light Walking

When Alec Holden turned ninety, he wagered a hundred British pounds with a betting agent that he'd live to be a hundred. Ten years later, in the prime of health, he returned to the "bookie" and collected a cool £25,000. A nice start to the second century of his life.

He was asked about the secret of his long life. "I keep breathing," he said. "If you stop breathing, you're in real trouble."*

Many Christians have stopped breathing. Not physically, but spiritually. Their experience is in a rut; they've stopped getting the fresh air that comes from learning from Jesus. The apostle John sat at Jesus' feet, and it was like inhaling great gulps of spiritual oxygen. Proclaiming the good news about life in Jesus energized John. His entire life and writings focus on Jesus and the theme of abundant and eternal life. Only John records the most-memorized words of Jesus: "For God so loved the world, that he gave his only begotten Son, that whosoever believeth in him should not perish, but have everlasting life" (John 3:16, KJV).

Immediately after he accepted Jesus' call to ministry by the Sea of Galilee, John got to see Jesus in action: healing the sick, casting out evil spirits, amazing people with His teaching (Mark 1:21–45).

---

* Mary Jordan, "Porridge-Eating Briton Cleans Up on Wager That He'd Reach 100," *Washington Post*, April 27, 2007.

His eyes opened to a new world far beyond splintered fishing boats, nets, and the daily catch. He caught a glimpse of what Jesus meant when He said he'd fish for people. From then on, John cast his net into the world—to catch and carry hope and healing to those who desperately needed it.

As he traveled with Jesus over the next few years, John experienced for himself His wonderful grace. Modestly declining to name himself in his own book, John refers to himself indirectly as the one Jesus loved (see John 13:23; 19:26; 20:2; 21:7, 20).

## Master lessons

On one occasion John and his brother, James, approached Jesus with a special request: " 'Let one of us sit at your right and the other at your left in your glory' " (Mark 10:37). In other words, when Jesus set up His earthly kingdom, would He please make sure they had the seats of honor?

It's not hard to imagine how indignant the other disciples felt when they heard that James and John had broken ranks in order to promote their own agenda (Mark 10:41). Why should James and John get special treatment? Why were they more worthy? The jostling for position continued.

Ironically, it was all for nothing. The disciples had everything backwards. They thought Jesus' kingdom would be political; thus, they didn't want to miss out on any of the fame or power.

What did Jesus teach them? He told them this was the sort of behavior you'd expect in the political world, from rulers and high officials, but certainly not from His followers. If they wanted to be great, they should act like servants and slaves. Even Jesus Himself didn't come to be served, but to serve (Mark 10:42–45). He came to give His life for the world.

On another occasion, James and John were upset because people in a Samaritan village didn't offer hospitality to Jesus. Their defense of Jesus was commendable; their tempers weren't. They asked Jesus if they should call down fire from heaven and destroy the villagers. That would teach them a lesson. (Of course, it wouldn't really. They'd all be dead.)

Jesus turned and rebuked John and his brother: " 'You do not know what kind of spirit you are of, for the Son of Man did not come to destroy men's lives, but to save them' " (see footnote on Luke 9:55, 56).

What a contrast between Jesus and His disciples. What a lesson for John to learn. And the biblical record shows that he did learn it. Later, after Philip established the Christian church in Samaria, John returned there with Peter. When they arrived, they prayed that the new believers would receive the Holy Spirit, and after spending some time teaching them, Peter and John returned to Jerusalem.

What did they do on their way home? They preached in Samaritan villages (Acts 8:25). Perhaps they even preached in the one John had wanted to fire-bomb not long before. What a dramatic change. From wannabe murderer to missionary. The former "Son of Thunder" would later write, "Anyone who does not love remains in death. Anyone who hates his brother is a murderer, and you know that no murderer has eternal life in him. This is how we know what love is: Jesus Christ laid down his life for us. And we ought to lay down our lives for our brothers" (1 John 3:14–16).

No more vying for power and position: "Do not love the world or anything in the world. If anyone loves the world, the love of the Father is not in him. . . . The world and its desires pass away, but the man who does the will of God lives forever" (1 John 2:15, 17). After the Resurrection, Jesus appeared to John and the disciples and gave them a clear commission: " 'As the Father has sent me, I am sending you' " (John 20:21) and gave them the gift of the Holy Spirit (verse 22). At Pentecost the Holy Spirit came powerfully, and John was never the same.

Luke describes how, on one occasion, John and Peter were walking up the temple steps to pray. A crippled man asked for money. They told him they didn't have any silver or gold, but they had something better. Peter healed him (Acts 3:4–8).

Soon after, they were both thrown into prison for teaching about Jesus and then taken to the Sanhedrin. There they gave a powerful testimony that shocked their audience (Acts 4:13).

## Key themes

If there was one thing John wanted people to know, it was that Jesus Christ brings eternal life. He is the " 'light of the world' " (John 9:5); " 'the way and the truth and the life' " (John 14:6); "full of grace and truth" (John 1:14). That conviction motivated John's entire life and mission.

John stresses how Jesus came and personally brought life to us. He "made his dwelling" among us and became human to reveal God's love (John 1:14). Of course, John knew full well that he was challenging the Gnostics of his day. For them, flesh was corrupt and evil. The only thing of value was the world of the spirit. And for a god to take on a physical body would be a total abomination.

But John would have nothing of that nonsense. He tells how the Son of God put on human flesh and died a physical death because of our sin. And, even more surprising, through His death Jesus brings life.

Scripture often uses the images of shepherds caring for sheep. In Ezekiel, God rebukes the " ' "shepherds of Israel who only take care of themselves!" ' " He asks, " ' "Should not shepherds take care of the flock?" ' " (Ezekiel 34:2). He adds, " ' "You have not strengthened the weak or healed the sick or bound up the injured. You have not brought back the strays or searched for the lost. You have ruled them harshly and brutally" ' " (Ezekiel 34:4).

The poet John Milton takes up this theme in his poem *Lycidas,* when he describes spiritual shepherds who don't do their job: "The hungry sheep look up, and are not fed."

In contrast, God says, " ' "I myself will search for my sheep and look after them. . . . I will search for the lost and bring back the strays. I will bind up the injured and strengthen the weak" ' " (verses 11, 16).

For John, following Jesus was a life-giving mission. His task, the task of all Christians, was to bring to hungry, dying sheep new life from Jesus. In His story of the sheep and the sheepfold, Jesus talks about thieves who come to steal and kill sheep. In contrast, He says, " 'I have come that they may have life, and have it to the full' " (John 10:10). It's perhaps no accident that in the closing verses of his Gospel, John again returns to this theme. He's the only biblical writer who records Jesus instructing Peter three times to feed His sheep.

## On the island of Patmos

More than fifty years after the Christian church was organized, the apostle John was still alive. He'd seen much, learned much. He'd given his life for the gospel. He'd seen Jerusalem destroyed and the temple reduced to rubble.

The terrible wave of persecution against Christians hit him as well. He was taken to Rome, tried, and thrown into a cauldron of boiling oil. But he survived and was exiled to the island of Patmos.

Here God revealed many wonders to him, including a vision that consumed his heart and soul, a vision of what would happen when Jesus returned. For the apostle John, the promise of Christ's second coming was a lifeline to which he desperately clung. He writes, "Then I saw a new heaven and a new earth, for the first heaven and the first earth had passed away, and there was no longer any sea" (Revelation 21:1).

These words are so familiar to us that we can easily miss the pathos, the heart-gripping emotion. The apostle John had seen so much, endured so much, from the Sea of Galilee to the middle of the Aegean Sea.

Here in the Greek islands, John was surrounded by water. For him it was a familiar scene, but he didn't look on it with the eyes of an old fisherman. He didn't look on it like today's sun-loving tourists who love to dive into Patmos's crystalline waters. He looked on it as a wall, an impenetrable barrier, between him and the Christian community he loved. He looked on it as a curse that imprisoned, a curse that separated him from his loved ones.

We can only imagine how his heart nearly burst as he saw the vision of a new heaven and a new earth replacing this old earth. *And there would be no more sea!* No more separation. It would be the ultimate homecoming for John. He described in more detail this wonderful vision, "I saw the Holy City, the new Jerusalem, coming down out of heaven from God, prepared as a bride beautifully dressed for her husband" (Revelation 21:2).

I've been married for many years. My hair is graying. I'm a lot slower than I used to be in many ways. I have aches and pains where I never used to. My baby daughter has a better memory than I do.

But I'll never forget the sight of my beautiful bride, Bettina, on our wedding day. I'll never forget the vision of her walking toward me through the garden where we held the ceremony.

And John could never forget his vision of the New Jerusalem coming down to earth "prepared as a bride beautifully dressed." "And I heard a loud voice from the throne saying, 'Now the dwelling of God is with men, and he will live with them. They will be his people, and God himself will be with them and be their God' " (Revelation 21:3).

Jesus' second coming will herald a new era of wonderful reconciliation in this place, a place with no more separation, "no more sea." The parallels with Jesus' first coming are clear. John tells us that when Jesus came to earth, He dwelt among us. John witnessed it. He was part of it. And now with all his heart he longed to see Him again.

For John, the Second Coming wasn't just some theoretical event in the distant future. No. It was everything he'd lived and worked for. It would be a homecoming. It would be reconciliation with His wonderful Jesus whom he loved with all his heart, mind, and soul. "He will wipe every tear from their eyes. There will be no more death or mourning or crying or pain, for the old order of things has passed away" (Revelation 21:4).

Again, hear the pathos in John's voice. He wasn't talking about hypothetical pain here. He wasn't talking about imagined mourning or tears. He had tears in his own eyes that he longed for Jesus to wipe away forever. He had pain in his own heart that wouldn't go away until Jesus returned. He'd seen the dreadful persecution of Christians by the Romans. He'd experienced it himself. And he longed with every part of his being for that wonderful day when Jesus would make everything right.

Now, after two thousand more years of the great cosmic conflict between good and evil, a lot more needs to be set right. Every day we see new results of the cosmic conflict between light and darkness. And like it or not, we can't be just spectators. The battleground goes right through our hearts. Each of us is either building up the wall of darkness or expanding the territory of light.

## Whatever happened to sin?

John knew the power of sin. He devoted his life to showing people how to escape its clutches. Today, it's not fashionable to talk about sin. It's not politically correct to mention wickedness. Our postmodern society prefers to discuss different "preferences," "tolerance," and how good people really are. Visit the New Age section of your local bookstore. Millions of people are buying books and DVDs on discovering the god within and on unleashing our innate goodness. But the last thing we need is another slick millionaire self-help guru telling us how wonderful we are.

Any pop-psychology or New Age babble that ignores the concept of sin isn't just adulterated garbage; it's dangerous. The Bible, as always, gives us the truth: " 'The human heart is the most deceitful of all things, and desperately wicked. Who really knows how bad it is?' " (Jeremiah 17:9, NLT).

I came across this New Age quote: "You have the inner strength and inner courage of victorious armies." The apostle John would be the first to tell us: "No, you don't. You're weak, you're vacillating. You need something more. You need a Savior from outside yourself who can lead you from the darkness into His wonderful light. A Savior who will one day return to make all wrongs right."

John records Jesus as saying that people " 'loved darkness instead of light because their deeds were evil. Everyone who does evil hates the light' " (John 3:19, 20).

One night, when I was a kid, my mother was ready to go to bed. Dad was still working in his study. She went out of the bedroom for something, and I crept into the darkened bedroom, stood beside the door, and put my hand over the light switch.

I loved the darkness because my deed was going to be evil. A few minutes later, Mom came through the door and went to turn on the light switch. What she felt instead was a warm hand in the darkness.

She screamed loudly to my dad. "Ernie! Ernie!" she cried.

Suddenly the joy evaporated with the sight of my suffering mother, and I was the one who ended up in tears. There's no lasting joy in the darkness. We can be taken from darkness into light because Jesus has brought His light into our darkness. But to a certain extent, it's like trying to look at the stars when you're in a city. As the apostle John knew so well, the full revelation of Jesus' light won't occur until He returns.

## Walking in the light

Growing up in a strong Adventist family, I was taught right from wrong. I have very positive memories of the right. Friday nights for me were light-filled times of great happiness. It was a time when the entire family would be together. The house would be spotlessly clean, I was bathed, I'd be wearing freshly laundered pajamas, Sabbath music would be playing, and I'd have a good book to read.

And every Friday night, Mom would cook hot soup with fresh bread. Potato soup was my favorite. I remember discussing with my brother a deep existential question. If we had the choice one Friday night of either having the delights of a box of chocolates or the comfort of Mom's Friday night soup, which would we choose? We came down on the side of the soup.

Friday nights are still a great joy. They're like walking in light. It's no surprise that observant Jews light Sabbath candles on Friday evening and, with great sorrow, extinguish them at the close of Sabbath. The salvation God offers lights a candle in our lives. But this candle never has to be put out. It's a guarantee that when He returns we'll be counted among those who'll be taken into His eternal light.

Have you had the light of God's love and forgiveness fill your life? Do you know what it means to move from darkness to light?

You don't have to go through some elaborate ritual, pay penance, make a pilgrimage, or try to make yourself good before you can ask God for forgiveness and a fresh start. Just open your heart to God. You may not hear the angels singing, and you may still feel bad and guilty, but just accept the fact that God has forgiven you. Eventually you'll know the "peace that passes all understanding."

Once we've experienced the love and the forgiveness and the grace and the joy, our lives will never be the same. Paul writes, "For you were once darkness, but now you are light in the Lord" (Ephesians 5:8). That means we live as children of the light. That means we live in goodness, righteousness, truth, and "what pleases the Lord" (Ephesians 5:9, 10).

John says, "Anyone who claims to be in the light but hates his brother is still in the darkness. Whoever loves his brother lives in the light" (1 John 2:9, 10).

When we step into the light, it makes a difference to our lives. Not only does God heal our past, He gives us strength for the future. We can walk confidently in the light as His sons and daughters, confident in His love and acceptance. We follow His commands not to make Him love us but because He already does.

## Hallelujah chorus

From his Patmos prison John describes his vision: "He who was seated on the throne said, 'I am making everything new!' Then he said, 'Write this down, for these words are trustworthy and true' " (Revelation 21:5).

Trustworthy and true. We hold no doubt that one day the cosmic war will end, God's light will pierce the grave's darkness and, as John Donne wrote, "Death, thou shalt die." We don't know the day or the hour, but He will come.

What are you and I doing in the days leading up to that day? Can we sing with enthusiasm, "This world is not my home"? Or are we too comfortable here? On whose side will we be found when Jesus returns?

Are we on the side of the One who shone light into darkness when He was resurrected two thousand years ago? In the choices we daily make, are we enlisting on the side of good or evil, of light or darkness? God will conduct a spiritual war-crimes tribunal, and the father of lies will confront the final truth. We'll all reap the consequences of our choices. The apostle John will join in loudly singing the deliverance song of Moses and the Lamb.

> Babies will snuggle once again in their mothers' arms.
> All suffering will cease. Forever.
> All wars will stop. Forever.
> No more crying. Forever.
> Only joy.
> And He shall reign forever and ever. Hallelujah.

# CHAPTER 8

# Peter: In the Presence of the Lord

One evening I knelt to pray before bed. Through my tiredness I began praising God. Suddenly it hit me that instead of saying, "It's a privilege to be Your son," I'd said, "It's a *pleasure* to be Your son." I thought about what I'd "accidentally" prayed and realized it was the truth. It *is* a pleasure, not just a privilege, to be called the son or daughter of God.

Many people follow God because they think it's the right thing to do. They follow Him, perhaps, for the hope of eternal reward, hoping that a heavenly paradise will compensate for any difficulties down here. Perhaps they do it out of a sense of duty. Perhaps they've been intellectually convinced, but it hasn't altered their lives.

Before Pentecost, Peter probably felt privileged to be Jesus' disciple. He respected Jesus and learned from Him. But was following Jesus a pleasure? He must have harbored misgivings and, at the very last, denied Jesus, embarrassed at being identified as His disciple.

But when Peter realized what he'd done, "he went outside and wept bitterly" (Luke 22:62). Mark says he "broke down" (Mark 14:72). These sad verses echo Judas's betrayal of Jesus. John, who was there, describes Judas leaving the upper room after he'd decided to sell out Jesus. He adds an interesting detail—"and it was night" (John 13:30). Not only was it dark outside; darkness consumed Judas's mind.

Both Judas and Peter felt guilt. Matthew says that when Judas saw Jesus condemned, he was "seized with remorse" (Matthew 27:3). But that's where the comparison ends and contrast begins. Responding to his guilt, Judas went and hanged himself (verse 5); Peter repented and changed his life. When Peter died decades later, it wasn't at his own hands. He died a martyr for his beloved Master and Friend.

The death of Jesus left Peter shocked, bewildered, and questioning. He'd never grasped that Jesus' mission was spiritual, not political. His warm dreams of an important position in an earthly kingdom were buried with Jesus in the cold tomb.

Jesus' resurrection changed everything. When the grieving women rushed from the tomb to report that Jesus had risen, the disciples didn't believe them. But something in Peter—a hint of his old impulsiveness, perhaps the urging of the Holy Spirit—made him leap up and run to the tomb. Then his friend John passed him in the outside lane! When they arrived, John "saw and believed" (John 20:8). Peter wasn't convinced. He wondered "to himself what had happened" (Luke 24:12).

When Jesus did finally appear to the disciples, He gave Peter a fresh start. Twice Jesus asked Peter whether he loved Him. Twice Peter answered "Yes." Each time Jesus responded, " 'Feed my lambs,' " " 'Take care of my sheep.' " When Jesus asked a third time whether Peter loved Him, a wounded Peter replied, " 'Lord, you know all things; you know that I love you.' " Again Jesus said, " 'Feed my sheep' " (John 21:15–17).

After Peter had denied Him three times, was Jesus now giving him the chance to affirm Him three times? Through these words, Jesus began the healing process that transformed Peter into a mighty leader of the Christian church. Jesus saw Peter's potential. He would harness Peter's strong emotions, impulsive faith, energy, and tremendous capacity for love to build and strengthen the body of believers.

Though Peter failed Him at a crucial time, Jesus forgave and trusted him. He ministered to Peter, showed how He valued him infinitely, and gave him a specific task—to care for His lambs, the new believers who would join the church. Finally, He instructed Peter, " 'Follow me!' " (John 21:19). After this personal commission, Peter devoted the rest of his life to one purpose: spiritual nurture of Jesus' flock, both inside and outside the fold.

## After Pentecost

Immediately after Jesus returned to heaven, Peter became one of the key leaders among the believers—numbering about a hundred twenty people in those early days. In Acts, Peter is usually named first in lists of the apostles, and he led the believers in choosing an apostle to replace Judas.

After Pentecost, when Peter stood and preached to the wondering crowd, the amazing transformation in his life became public (Acts 2:14–41). The Holy Spirit empowered his preaching as three thousand people accepted Jesus and were baptized.

Following Jesus had become a pleasure for Peter. His life was now fired by one mission—to share the love of His precious Savior. Nothing would stop him. In the years to come he would preach on city streets, in synagogues, and in prisons. He would help lead the church, heal the sick, and even raise the dead.

Later, temple guards seized Peter and John and threw them into jail. They had to defend themselves before the "rulers, elders and teachers of the law" in Jerusalem (Acts 4:5). But they didn't defend themselves; they defended Jesus.

Among the leaders in this hostile audience were Annas the high priest, his son-in-law Caiaphas, and other members of his family. From a worldly perspective, it was an uneven match. Two uneducated Galilean fishermen up against the religious elite—trained in the best schools, highly placed, and powerful.

But the apostles weren't intimidated. "Filled with the Holy Spirit," Peter spoke boldly about Jesus (Acts 4:8). The august audience was stunned. "When they saw the courage of Peter and John and realized that they were unschooled, ordinary men, they were astonished and they took note that these men had been with Jesus" (Acts 4:13).

What about us today? Can people tell that we've "been with Jesus"?

Some years ago I was sitting on a small plane flying from the island of Tasmania to the Australian mainland. A young man wearing outdoors-type clothing sat beside me. In Australia, we call people like him a "greenie"—an environmentalist.

Tasmania has some of the oldest, most spectacular virgin forest left in the world. Much of it carries a World Heritage listing. Over the years environmentalists and loggers have battled over what should or shouldn't be done to the trees. The young man next to me said he'd gone to Tasmania to join others in protesting against logging, and they'd had a face-to-face confrontation with developers.

When he discovered I was a Christian, he began talking about his sister, whom he said was also a Christian. Then he made a statement I'll never forget. "Yes, she's a committed Christian. She's really involved in her church and prays about everything. But she's not at all interested in helping with any social issues." He paused and then added sadly, "But she'll consult God about the color of her car."

Whether the greenies or the developers were right in this particular case is beside the point. This young man knew his sister was a Christian, but she had no social concern. She shared no interest, ironically, in her nonbelieving brother's efforts to preserve God's creation. Her beliefs didn't translate into behavior her brother could respect. He couldn't see evidence that she'd been with Jesus.

My grandmother shrank as she grew older. I was growing, she was shrinking, and one day I was taller. From then on, I called her "Shorty." I loved her so much. Her white curly hair was like wool. Propped up in an armchair, she'd often fall asleep and blow short bursts of breath out the corner of her mouth. My brother and I loved to tease her about that. She always took it in good fun.

Nana's eyes plagued her as glaucoma slowly attacked her sight. I watched, fascinated, as she put drops in her eyes each day. I looked into her large watering eyes. Would she go blind? Nana would hold her large-print King James Version Bible up close to her eyes and read with a magnifying glass for hours, through the pain.

Finally her health failed, and she moved into a nursing home. Her frail, small body lay on top of a tall metal bed with crisp white sheets. I held her bony hand and thought about her life. Widowed in her forties, she was left destitute. Yet she raised her two sons in God's love. They both became teachers and then pastors.

One day I went to visit Nana in the nursing home. I slowly pushed open her door a little to check on her. She wasn't in her bed. Somehow she'd climbed off her tall metal bed onto the cold, linoleum floor. She was kneeling, eyes closed. This frail, dying woman was bowing before her Creator and Savior. There was never any question in my mind that Nana had been with Jesus. She was a woman of God and had spent plenty of time with Jesus.

## A transformed life

Peter had a long and bitter experience trying to do things his own way. He would never forget sinking into the dark waters after taking his eyes off Jesus (Matthew 14:22–32), Jesus rebuking him for trying to do things his own way (Matthew 16:22–24), his rash words on the Mount of Transfiguration (Matthew 17:1–13), falling asleep in Gethsemane (Matthew 26:36–46), and impulsively severing the ear of the high priest's servant (John 18:10, 11).

His memories of his actions leading up to Jesus' death must have haunted him. Extravagant boasts of faithfulness followed by a shocking and brutal denial. A look from his Lord flickering over and over in his mind like a looping video clip.

But the Cross had brought the bragger to his knees. As his spiritual commitment increased, so did his humility. When Peter visited the house of Cornelius, a highly respected centurion, Cornelius "fell at his feet in reverence" (Acts 10:25). Peter wouldn't accept the tribute. " 'Stand up,' he said, 'I am only a man myself' " (verse 26).

He was still human. In fact, he publicly clashed with Paul, his fellow apostle and leader. "When Peter came to Antioch," Paul wrote, "I opposed him to his face, because he was clearly in the wrong" (Galatians 2:11). This was just after Peter had given Paul "the right hand of fellowship" (verse 9).

They clashed over something central to the church's mission—how to relate to Gentiles who were becoming Christians. Following his experience with Cornelius, Peter had begun regularly fellowshiping and eating with Gentile Christians. But now, said Paul, Peter had stopped eating with them because "he was afraid of those who belonged to the circumcision group" in Jerusalem (verse 12). Paul felt Peter was being hypocritical (verse 13). He probably was.

Some commentators suggest that the "circumcision group" were non-Christian Jews who were upset to hear that this prominent Christian leader was eating with Gentiles. Because of Peter's behavior, the "circumcision group" could have been threatening the church and its witness; Peter may have been acting to protect the church.

## Breaking old habits

Peter's fame as a healer and miracle worker spread quickly. People placed the sick where his shadow would fall on them as he walked by (Acts 5:15). He healed sick people for the same reason Jesus did—because he had compassion on them. And he also used the miracles as a launching pad to talk about Jesus.

Some get nervous about mixing Christian witness with physical care. They fear we'll attract "rice Christians," those who pay lip service to Christianity to get benefits from the "missionary"—a bowl of rice, physical healing, or some other reward. (Of course, how many of us can claim that we came to Jesus with only the highest, noblest motives? Did an everlasting heaven attract us? Did we seek to avoid eternal death? Aren't these motives in the same category as wanting a bowl of rice to avoid starvation?)

Certainly it's wrong even to hint that someone must accept our message before we give him or her physical care. Our humanitarian work should show no-strings-attached compassion. But does that mean we should separate humanitarian care and Christian witness?

Jesus cheerfully fed the crowds and also taught them about the kingdom. When He sent out Peter and the other disciples to minister, He told them to teach and heal. Jesus takes us in our weakness, our sinfulness, our confused and mixed intentions. He takes us from our self-interested, narrow-visioned state and teaches us more about Himself. He broadens our perspective, purifies our tainted motives.

That's precisely what He did with Peter. Peter could never have imagined, as he repaired his glistening fishing nets by Galilee, that one day he'd stand among government leaders, powerfully declaring his faith. But Jesus had bigger plans for Peter and all His disciples: " 'You will be my witnesses in Jerusalem, and in all Judea and Samaria, and to the ends of the earth' " (Acts 1:8).

Jesus trained His disciples for mission: "Go ye therefore, and teach all nations, baptizing them in the name of the Father, and of the Son, and of the Holy Ghost: Teaching them to observe all things whatsoever I have commanded you: and, lo, I am with you alway, even unto the end of the world. Amen" (Matthew 28:19, 20, KJV).

Often we neglect the opening and crucial words to this passage: " 'All authority in heaven and on earth has been given to me. Therefore go . . .' " (verses 18, 19). Jesus' followers can go into all the world, teach all nations, and make disciples *because* Jesus has all authority in heaven and earth. Because He has that authority, He gives it to His followers. As Paul says, "You have been given fullness in Christ, who is the head over every power and authority" (Colossians 2:10).

Through a vision Peter learned that "all the world" included Gentiles. This was unheard of. As a good Jew, Peter wasn't supposed to visit a Gentile's home or even entertain Gentile visitors. But Peter answered God's call and traveled to the house of Cornelius, in Caesarea. There he threw out past rules for the sake of the gospel— " 'God has shown me that I should not call any man impure or unclean. So when I was sent for, I came without raising any objection' " (Acts 10:28, 29). The rest is history. Peter ministered to the Gentiles in that household; "the Holy Spirit came on all who heard the message," and the floodgates opened for the good news to go to the entire world (Acts 10:44).

Whenever someone tries something innovative in mission, some will criticize. I still have in my e-mail files a message from a pastor working on the front line of mission. For many years he'd lived and worked in some of the most difficult and challenging areas of the world. He tried new and creative methods for reaching people, and many accepted Jesus through his work.

But toward the end of his ministry he wrote to me suggesting that he might resign to help "defuse some of the controversy flying around." I thought this was terribly sad. It's hard enough working to reach "unreached" people without the added burden of criticism from "the saints."

Translating the good news into terms people can understand often means doing things different from the norm. It may mean changing established ways and methods. It may mean altering schedules and rituals and some of those precious but ultimately unproductive "we've always done it this way" things.

So Peter was criticized: "The circumcised believers criticized him and said, 'You went into the house of uncircumcised men and ate with them' " (Acts 11:2, 3). But we must give the critics credit. They didn't just talk behind his back; they spoke to him directly about their concerns. After he explained what had happened, "they had no further objections and praised God, saying, 'So then, God has granted even the Gentiles repentance unto life' " (Acts 11:18).

So beautifully understated. The critics became supporters and opened the door to a defining moment in the history of the Christian church.

I'm so glad for innovative, Holy Spirit–driven people in the church who are trying creative new ways to translate the good news into terms people can understand. At first we may not fully understand the reasons for their style or approach. And the innovators may make mistakes. But who doesn't?

I'm glad for church members who support new strategies and who don't just sit back and criticize. Who, when they understand the purpose, throw out their objections and praise God. What a mistake to have stood in the way of what God wanted to do in the days of Peter and the other apostles. What a shame to stand in the way of what God wants to do today.

Peter's story gives us hope. Most of us identify with him because he was so human. Without too much imagination we can see ourselves trying to walk on water and losing faith, making inane comments on the Mount of Transfiguration, even denying our Lord, given the right circumstances.

Recently, I was glancing through the *Washington Post*'s weekly listing of religious worship services in the Washington area. One heading caught my attention: "Imagine a Religion That Puts Its Faith in You!"*

*That's supposed to be a selling point?* I thought.

Peter discovered that his life changed only when he transferred his faith from himself to Jesus. That's always when serving Jesus becomes a pleasure.

---

* *Washington Post,* November 10, 2007.

# CHAPTER 9

# Peter: We Tread the Ground

Some years ago, I visited the Central Coast Community Church, a Seventh-day Adventist church in Wyong, on the east coast of Australia. It began as a church plant, supported by Global Mission, with a mission to reach people who don't attend any church and who have no background in Christianity. My brother, Wayne, is the pastor.

I attended the children's Sabbath School, full of kids straight off the street who'd never before stepped into a church. It was the loudest, craziest Sabbath School I've ever attended. The teachers fought to keep some sort of discipline and didn't spend much time discussing the finer theological points of the week's lesson.

Halfway through the class, the little girl sitting next to me suddenly threw her hand into the air and called out, "How did Jesus die?"

She paused a moment and added, "I hope He got shot."

I don't think anyone else heard her. But it hit me hard. I looked at her. She had no idea about the life and death of Jesus. Perhaps the only time she'd ever heard His name was when her parents were swearing. No doubt the bits and pieces she heard in Sabbath School got mixed up in her head with Hollywood action DVDs she'd seen—and she blurted out "I hope He got shot."

A whole generation in Western countries has little or no knowledge of Jesus or the Bible. We used to pray for children in mission fields such as Africa, India, and China. We'd better start praying for ways to reach the children in Western mission fields too.

When Otis Moss III graduated from Yale Divinity School, he began working with former gang members and drug dealers in Connecticut. One day he was talking about amazing grace, and a man asked him, "Who is she?" That was a turning point for Moss, and his ministry would never be the same. Moss realized he had to totally change the way he talked and ministered if he was to have any hope of reaching people for Jesus.

Naturally, we're all more comfortable talking with people who share our language, culture, and beliefs. We don't have to work as hard to find common ground. We relax more. We don't have to fear breaking some crucial taboo or giving unwitting offense.

The apostle Peter was most comfortable interacting with fellow Jews. That's the culture he knew. In fact, he had virtually no experience with other people. Sure, he'd seen Jesus working with Gentiles. But his personal contact with non-Jews had been limited or nonexistent. He'd certainly never shared a meal with anyone other than a Jew.

But all that changed with his rooftop vision and groundbreaking visit to the home of Cornelius. His world opened up to a new vista of spiritual need—people who'd never heard about clean or unclean foods, circumcision, or the Ten Commandments. Little girls who didn't know how or why Jesus died. Men who'd never heard of amazing grace.

Most of Peter's personal ministry was devoted to his fellow Jews, but the church soon started reaching out to Gentiles who didn't know the first thing about Jewish faith and traditions, about Jesus or God's Word. With these people, it was like starting from the beginning—teaching the basics, the ABCs of salvation.

## Prepare for action

Despite what we may think of Cuba's communist regime, or its president Fidel Castro, this island nation ran one of the world's most successful literacy campaigns in the early 1960s. More than a quarter million people gave up work and studies to volunteer their time to help fellow Cubans learn to read and write. At the start of the campaign, more than 25 percent of Cubans were illiterate; at the end, less than 4 percent were.

How did this educational miracle occur in such a short time? The methods were based on the controversial theories of a Christian educator, Paulo Freire. But the bottom line was simple: thousands volunteered.*

In many ways the Cuban literacy campaign parallels the outreach of the early Christian church, which the apostle Peter influenced in so many ways.

*1. A clear mission.* The motto of the Cuban literacy campaign was, "If you know, teach; if you don't know, learn." The mission was simple—teach people to read and write. Likewise, the early Christian church had a clear mission: to tell the world about Jesus.

His parting words to the disciples were the blueprint, the reason for being, for the Christian church. We know these words as the "Great Commission" (Matthew 28:18–20). Without it, the church would have turned into an inward-looking club for believers, and it may have lasted a few years.

Peter urged his fellow believers to reach out to others and to "live such good lives among the pagans that, though they accuse you of doing wrong, they may see your good deeds and glorify God on the day he visits us" (1 Peter 2:12).

*2. Lay people involved.* The Cubans didn't leave teaching to the literacy experts. People from all walks of life got involved. Schools shut down for eight months, and even school children (from the sixth grade up) joined the campaign as teachers.

Likewise, Christian witness isn't the specialized responsibility of "professional evangelists." It's the task of every church member. In fact, Peter called all church members "a royal priesthood, a holy nation, a people belonging to God, that you may declare the praises of him who called you out of darkness into his wonderful light" (1 Peter 2:9, 10).

---

* In case anyone is wondering, this is not a political endorsement of Cuba's communist government!

This was a fundamental doctrine of the Reformation, and it's a vital part of our spiritual heritage. God has given spiritual authority to all believers to be His witnesses. It's not something we leave to paid clergy.

This means we're God's witnesses no matter where we work. A carpenter sharing his faith with fellow workers is just as much a witness as a public evangelist holding a series of meetings. A doctor showing God's love to her patients is just as much a witness as a pastor preaching a sermon Sabbath morning.

The strength of the Cuban literacy campaign was the way it mobilized people in a common task. The strength of the church is in rallying all its members in living and telling the good news.

*3. Despite threats.* The first literacy training session began near the capital, Havana, on April 15, 1961, with a group of a thousand student volunteers. Two days later, on the other side of the island, the Bay of Pigs invasion of Cuba began. Despite the military threat, the campaign continued.

The early Christian church suffered many attacks. Peter himself was persecuted and, at the end of his life, was crucified. He didn't feel worthy to die like his Master, so he requested to be crucified upside down.

Rather than dampening evangelistic zeal, persecution strengthened the witness of the early Christian church. Peter wrote, "But even if you should suffer for what is right, you are blessed. . . . Always be prepared to give an answer to everyone who asks you to give the reason for the hope that you have" (1 Peter 3:14, 15).

He added, "Dear friends, do not be surprised at the painful trial you are suffering, as though something strange were happening to you. But rejoice that you participate in the sufferings of Christ, so that you may be overjoyed when his glory is revealed" (1 Peter 4:12, 13).

*4. The personal touch.* Leaders carefully planned each phase of the Cuban literacy campaign. During the day, many volunteer teachers worked beside people, building the trust and confidence of older citizens who became more willing to learn.

Today Global Mission pioneers around the world know the importance of building trust and friendship. Since 1993 thousands of pioneers have modeled the incarnational ministry of Jesus. Pioneers are lay people, usually young, who go into a new area to establish an Adventist congregation. They receive only a small stipend and live among their own people. They know the culture, speak the language, and live at the same socioeconomic level as the people they seek to reach.

As a young pioneer, Budiman Soreng witnessed men walking around town with the decapitated heads of their enemies dangling from their hands. He was working in the Bengkayang area of Kalimantan on the Indonesian side of the island of Borneo where there'd been fierce tribal warfare—complete with beheadings and cannibalism. Budiman established three groups of believers and then became a district pastor supervising a team of Global Mission pioneers in the same region.

Pioneering for the gospel was in Budiman's blood (his father, too, was a Global Mission pioneer). He says his first task, when he arrived in Bengkayang, was to "study the situation," the place, and the people. Next he started to make friends with Animists, Muslims, and Chinese Buddhists, as well as other Christians. "I played football with the people, went jogging in the mornings, and worked with them in the rice fields," he says. "At midnight I prayed, 'Lord, first work in my heart. Then I can work with the people. Let me say what Jesus would say.' "

Budiman began visiting homes, talking with the people in their own dialect and sharing from the Bible. More than two hundred people were baptized, and with the help of four other pioneers, five new areas were opened up.

The key to successful outreach, Budiman told me, is to be humble. "We have an expression here—'we tread the ground,' " he said. "That means 'we come here, we are like the people here.' "*

What a beautiful word picture of what Jesus did for us! He came to earth and "trod the ground." Do we try to witness without "tread-

---

* For more information, pictures, and stories of Global Mission pioneers, visit http://www.global-mission.org.

ing the ground"? Do we see witnessing as some kind of noncontact sport? Do we rely on tracts, radio, television, and "professional evangelists" to do our witnessing rather than living, working, and playing among people of the community, becoming one with them, making friends, and sharing God's love?

Peter knew what it was to "tread the ground" for Jesus. When Cornelius sent for help, Peter didn't delegate the job to someone else. He personally traveled to Caesarea to witness to Cornelius and his household. It may have gone against every cultural and religious bone in his body, but he stayed in the Gentile's house, ate with Gentiles, and shared with them. They, and he, were never the same again.

*5. Making the message meaningful.* Paulo Freire, whose theories drove the Cuban literacy campaign, spoke about praxis—connecting actions to values. It's not enough just to teach letters and words. They have to be meaningful, not just marks on paper. They have to connect with what's important in people's lives and make them hungry to learn more.

So the Cuban teachers used politically charged lessons and pictures (perhaps better described as propaganda), drawing examples from rural life. Pictures were carefully chosen to awaken the learners' interests. They addressed issues such as hygiene, nutrition, justice, and having enough to feed your family. One lesson, for example, said, "Let's first read and then write: 'The fishing cooperative helps the fishermen. They sell fish in the cooperative. Daniel helps to sell. The money is for everyone. The fishermen are no longer exploited. Now the fishermen live better lives. New lives for the fishermen.' Copy in your best handwriting: 'Daniel helps to sell.' "*

In the same way, it's not enough to just give an intellectual nod toward a set of Christian beliefs. They can't be just a list in a book. They need to connect with life. If they don't, they'll have no power, and something else will take their place.

I once spoke with a young, single mother who soon learned I was a Seventh-day Adventist. "Oh, I'm [she named another

---

* "The Little Engine That Dialectically Must," *Harper's,* February 2004.

denomination]," she said. "But I don't attend anymore." And then, turning to her child, she added, "And I'm not going to prejudice Emily in any way. I want her to wait until she's old enough to make up her own mind."

The problem is, Emily won't grow up in a vacuum. Nobody and nothing else will show her mother's tolerance. The television in the corner of the family room isn't going to say, "I won't prejudice Emily until she's old enough to make decisions for herself." The popular music industry won't vow, "I'm not going to influence Emily until she can make up her own mind." And the Internet surely isn't going to make any such promises.

In Deuteronomy 11, God says, " 'Fix these words of mine in your hearts and minds; tie them as symbols on your hands and bind them on your foreheads. Teach them to your children, talking about them when you sit at home and when you walk along the road, when you lie down and when you get up. Write them on the doorframes of your houses and on your gates' " (verses 18–20).

Of course, God is talking more than literally here. His words have little value if they stay as symbols on our hands and foreheads, or just written on doorframes and gates. They have to be demonstrated in love and obedience to Him.

Peter wrote, "Make every effort to add to your faith goodness; and to goodness, knowledge; and to knowledge, self-control; and to self-control, perseverance; and to perseverance, godliness; and to godliness, brotherly kindness; and to brotherly kindness, love. For if you possess these qualities in increasing measure, they will keep you from being ineffective and unproductive in your knowledge of our Lord Jesus Christ" (2 Peter 1:5–8).

I remember studying these words many years ago. I was having worship in a cabin at Yarahapinni, the youth camp of the North New South Wales Conference, in Australia. It's a beautiful place, right on the beach. There was just a small group of us—including Pastor Eric White, our beloved youth director and a true spiritual leader. Together we discussed this passage.

Suddenly it hit me: *It's possible to have knowledge of Jesus and still be "ineffective and unproductive."* I can memorize the entire Scrip-

88

tures without it touching my life. I can even graduate top of the class in theological seminary and still be "ineffective and unproductive" in my knowledge.

We can know every doctrine and still oppose God. We can attend church every Sabbath but be a horrible neighbor. We can have the most impressive satellite TV network and be the coldest church on earth. We can be vegetarians and act like pigs.

James reminds us that even the devils believe in one God (James 2:19), but they remain devils. Beliefs must change our lives.

Often those who adhere most rigidly to doctrines overlook the spirit of the Jesus to whom the doctrines point. In the early 1980s in Australia, many Seventh-day Adventists took the hymn "Onward Christian Soldiers" literally as they battled over theology. At times, on both sides, love got lost in the clouds of correct-doctrine gunfire. Thousands were spiritually injured.

One church member stopped to say Hello to the senior elder in the church foyer one Sabbath morning. The elder glared, reached into his pocket, and handed him a coin.

"Here," he said, walking off. "Give me a call when your theology has changed." No doubt this elder believed all the church's fundamental doctrines. But today, yet another family no longer worships in the Seventh-day Adventist Church.

Peter writes, "Therefore, prepare your minds for action" (1 Peter 1:13). Our beliefs must connect with our lives. We must act what we believe. Peter had spent much of his life acting with an unprepared mind. But the Holy Spirit changed his life and prepared him for action. He now dedicated his life to sharing the good news of His wonderful Savior.

It was good news for Galilean fishermen. It's good news for those of us who've kept religious knowledge in our heads. And it's good news for little boys and girls who don't know about Jesus.

# CHAPTER 10

# Women: "Necessary to the Work of the Ministry"

Once while traveling through Samaria, Jesus met a woman. That sounds like a straightforward sentence, but at that time Jewish men weren't supposed to meet women in public. Especially Samaritan women. Especially adulterous Samaritan women.

They met at Jacob's well, a historic site near Sychar—once an important city with a temple to rival Jerusalem's (John 4:5, 6). In the heat of the day, in a dusty Samarian town, they talked together—the Son of God and a promiscuous woman shunned by good, upright citizens (some speculate she was drawing water at noon to avoid the gossip of those collecting water in the cooler hours of the morning). But there should be no surprise. After all, this is the Jesus who made friends with "sinners" and who said, " 'I have not come to call the righteous, but sinners to repentance' " (Luke 5:32).

Jesus' dialogue with this woman is the longest recorded conversation He ever had. Jesus looked beyond the surface. He saw past the woman's history and reputation to her deepest fears and longings. As Jesus talked with this prodigal daughter, He drew her to Himself. She was transformed.

When Jesus' disciples returned from gathering food, they were shocked to see Him talking publicly with a Samaritan woman. He didn't rebuke them for their prejudice. Instead, He described a

90

vision—fields that were white, ready for harvest. Of course, He wasn't giving them a lesson on farming; He was talking about a harvest of humanity—people ready to be brought into His kingdom.

As soon as she heard the "words of life" from Jesus, the Samaritan woman felt compelled to share them. She immediately left her water jar and ran to tell people about her encounter with the Water of Life. Through her testimony she sowed spiritual seed that yielded a great harvest when Philip later went to Samaria (Acts 8:5–25 and see *The Acts of the Apostles,* p. 106).

The Orthodox Church names the woman at the well Photini, meaning "equal to the apostles." Tradition says that after Jesus' death she was baptized and traveled to many regions to preach the good news about her Savior. She and her children—five daughters and two sons—were arrested and taken to Rome. There she witnessed to Emperor Nero's daughter, who became a believer. Eventually Photini's entire family were martyred.

A Byzantine hymn pays tribute to Photini:

> By the well of Jacob, O holy one,
> thou didst find the Water
> of eternal and blessed life;
> and having partaken
> thereof, O wise Photini,
> thou wentest forth proclaiming Christ, the Anointed One.*

Of course, we don't know the truth of this tradition. But we do know that a converted Samaritan woman was one of the first missionaries Jesus appointed.

Although biblical accounts of women are brief and women often appear only on the edges of the action, Jesus broke through the customs of His day to elevate them to a proper status. It's somehow appropriate that women were the first people to discover that Jesus had risen from the grave and the first group He asked to share the news of His resurrection (Matthew 28:10).

---

* http://orthodox.net/questions/samaritan_woman_1-a.txt.

## A missionary tradition

Some two thousand years later, in 1899, Ruby Ferris was born in rural Australia and grew up in a humble house with a dirt floor. She married Norman Ferris, and in their early twenties, they headed as Adventist missionaries to the Solomon Islands in the South Pacific. They faced incredible challenges, hardships, and joys. It was a long way from the Samaria of Jesus' time, but their mission was the same—to share the Water of Life with the spiritually thirsty.

Once Mrs. Ferris was asked to help a sick eighteen-month-old child who had been constipated for several days. But when Mrs. Ferris arrived at the village to help, the mother panicked and fled into the jungle. Mrs. Ferris wrote in her memoirs:

> Next morning I again visited the home where the sick child lived, and what I saw staggered me. The devil priest had been called in and with a knife had cut a gash fully an inch deep all around the buttocks of the child . . . which they said was to let the devil out. The little girl was only semi-conscious. I made a dressing of soothing ointment in the form of a napkin and remonstrated with the family on their foolishness. Not far away stood the devil priest, and he got a good tongue banging from me. I threatened to report him to the government. . . . Next morning before arriving at the village I could hear the cries of mourning from the house and knew that the child was dead with the mother still holding the body. I sat on the wooden slat that composed her bed and putting my arms around her told her how sorry I was. I asked her how many other children she had, and her reply was "This make'm four fellow he die finish." She had lost three other babies besides this one. . . . How badly they needed the healing power of the gospel of Christ. If only they would accept the waters of life so freely offered.*

---

\* Unpublished handwritten memoirs courtesy of Pastor Irwin Ferris, Ruby Ferris's son. You can read the full memoirs at www.AdventistMission.org.

On another occasion, malaria struck two of her children while her husband was away traveling. She had to walk six miles—carrying her children—to get help.

One night their mission boat hit a reef, and her three-year-old baby daughter, Norma, was flung into the waters. Divers searched the waters while Mrs. Ferris prayed and wept. Finally, after several minutes, Solomon Islander Pastor Kata Ragaso found the little girl, and they broke the surface, gulping air.

Despite years of hard, lonely labor, Mrs. Ferris felt she and her husband hadn't accomplished much for the gospel in the Solomons. In 1989, long after her husband's death, she was invited back for an anniversary celebration in one of the main areas where they'd helped establish new congregations. She was overjoyed to find seven churches with eighteen hundred members. And she met an old man who, in 1932, had been a "devil priest" and who had believed the devil had commissioned him to kill Norman Ferris with an axe. But instead of murdering Pastor Ferris, the man had become a Seventh-day Adventist and had remained faithful for more than fifty years.

Six years later, at age ninety-five, Mrs. Ferris again visited the Solomon Islands. As her boat approached the island of Guadalcanal, she rose early and—from the front of the ship—identified places where she and her husband had worked to establish mission stations. As the boat docked at Honiara Wharf, more than a thousand uniformed church members formed an honor guard to greet her. Tears came to her eyes as she said, "It must have been worthwhile after all."

Mrs. Ferris stands tall in a rich tradition of millions of dedicated Adventist women who have advanced God's kingdom on earth. Despite the fact that customs and culture have often treated women as inferior to men, silenced their voices, and discriminated against them—they've been faithful missionaries for God.*

---

* Most of the information on Adventist women in the following section comes from the Web site of the General Conference Adventist Women's Ministries department, http://wm.gc.adventist.org/Pages/women_distinguished_service.html, and *The Seventh-day Adventist Encyclopedia*, Review and Herald® Publishing Association, 2002.

In 1877, the General Conference of Seventh-day Adventists sent Maud Sisley as the first Adventist woman missionary to Europe. She helped Pastor J. N. Andrews with publishing work in Switzerland and then went to England as a Bible instructor and colporteur. She later married Charles Boyd, and in 1887 they traveled with the first group of Adventist missionaries to Africa. After her husband's death in 1898, Mrs. Boyd sailed to Australia, where she worked as a teacher and Bible instructor for twelve years.

In 1895 Georgia Burns went to India as a self-supporting missionary and worked there for nearly forty years. She set out for India with one dollar in her pocket before someone donated eighty dollars to her cause. She worked among the "secluded women"—who by custom lived totally isolated from their communities—and helped establish a girls' school in Calcutta. In 1903 she married Luther Burgess, and for thirty-two years they pioneered Adventist work among the Bengali-, Hindi-, Urdu-, and Khasi-speaking peoples.

After serving as a Bible worker in the Minnesota, Dakota, and Ohio conferences, Lucy Post, single and fifty years old, went to Argentina and Uruguay in the late 1890s as the first Adventist woman missionary to South America.

American Florence Keller was the first woman physician sent as an overseas missionary by the Adventist Church. She and her husband, Peter, also a doctor, worked in New Zealand from 1901 to 1919, where she served the Maori royal family. Florence was a keen cyclist and also traveled on horseback to treat patients in remote Maori communities. The *Dictionary of New Zealand Biography* recognizes her as a "social reformer" involved in community activity, local politics, educational causes, and the Women's Christian Temperance Union.*

Ana Stahl, a Swedish nurse and teacher, pioneered Adventist work in the Lake Titicaca region of Peru with her husband, Ferdinand. Arriving in the Peruvian Andes in 1909, they found an

---

* "A few years before her retirement in her mid nineties, Florence Keller was acclaimed the oldest practicing surgeon in the world." McKergow, Fiona, "Keller, Nettie Florence 1875-1974." *Dictionary of New Zealand Biography,* updated June 22, 2007, (http://www.dnzb.govt.nz).

oppressed Indian population. They labored among the poorest of the poor—the 95 percent indigenous population—and helped knock down barriers of race, religion, and social class. They founded chapels, clinics, markets, and the first coeducation school. The education system they established grew to two hundred schools surrounding Lake Titicaca, with tens of thousands of students. Through their faith, firmly rooted in the Bible, these Seventh-day Adventist missionaries started a social revolution in Peru. Then, in 1921, they went to the headwaters of the Amazon River, where they served another eighteen years.

Lottie Isbell, the first African American Adventist woman physician, married David Blake, a pastor and physician. Just before World War I, they went as self-supporting missionaries to Panama. From there they went on to serve also in Haiti and Jamaica.

Jessie Halliwell, a nurse, and her husband, Leo, went to Brazil in 1921 as medical missionaries. They labored there for thirty-eight years—thirty years along the Amazon River, utilizing the mission boat *Luziero* as an "aquatic clinic." They covered twelve thousand miles of river each year, and it's estimated that they treated more than a quarter million Brazilians and Indians. The Brazilian government awarded the Halliwells the distinguished National Order of the Southern Cross for their outstanding service.

In the same year that the Halliwells left for Brazil, British missionary Grace Clark traveled from England to East Africa. In Kenya, she established educational work for girls and then served as secretary-treasurer of the Kenya Union Mission for five years. Her tremendous work in translating the Bible into the Luo language, a translation that is still used today, led the British and Foreign Bible Society to appoint her a life member of that organization.

Helen Morton, a physician and medical director at California State University at Fullerton, California, in the late 1970s went as a medical missionary to Thailand, where she established a small hospital at Chiang Mai. This highly accomplished woman trekked through the hills and rode elephants to help the tribal people in the region. Her life of service came to a tragic end when she was murdered in 1981.

## Early Christian church

Women played a vital role in the early Christian church. A woman named Lydia who traded in purple cloth accepted Jesus through the apostle Paul's witness in Philippi. Details about her are brief: "The Lord opened her heart to respond to Paul's message. When she and the members of her household were baptized, she invited us to her home" (Acts 16:14, 15). Despite the demands of running her business, Lydia found time to share her faith, establish a house church, and provide hospitality to the apostles.

Lydia came from Thyatira, in the Roman province of Asia. Perhaps she was visiting Philippi for business purposes. Paul was supposed to be in Asia at that time, but the Holy Spirit had prevented him from going. Instead, he had traveled to Thyatira, where he shared the good news with Lydia. Had God chosen Lydia and her household to return to Asia to share the good news?

At one time Paul lived and worked in Corinth with Priscilla and her husband, Aquila, who were tentmakers (Acts 18:1–3). But they did more than just make tents. Paul described them as "my fellow workers in Christ Jesus" (Romans 16:3). Everywhere they went, Priscilla and Aquila turned their home into a house church (1 Corinthians 16:19; Romans 16:5). Their spiritual influence was strong, and Paul paid tribute to them: "They risked their lives for me. Not only I but all the churches of the Gentiles are grateful to them" (Romans 16:4).

Philip the evangelist's four unmarried daughters prophesied (Acts 21:9), which was a vital spiritual gift in the early church. Another woman, Phoebe, served as a minister.* Many other women in the early church were known for good works. Dorcas "was always doing good and helping the poor" (Acts 9:36); Tryphena and Tryphosa were "women who work hard in the Lord"; Persis was "another woman who has worked very hard in the Lord" (Romans 16:12).

---

* Most times this word is used in Scripture, the King James Version translates it as "minister" (other times it translates it as "servant" or "deacon"). So Paul could have meant that Phoebe was "a minister of the church" or "a deaconess of the church." Whatever the correct meaning, it is clear that Phoebe served the church.

## Women: "Necessary to the Work of the Ministry"

The Bible mentions other women specifically for their work in spreading the good news. Paul says that Euodia and Syntyche "contended at my side in the cause of the gospel" (Philippians 4:2, 3). He also refers to Apphia as one of the leaders of a house church (Philemon 2) and to Nympha, who also had a church in her house (Colossians 4:15).

Writing to the church in Corinth, Paul says that other apostles, as well as Jesus' brothers, took their wives on missionary journeys (1 Corinthians 9:5). Some say the correct translation of this verse means that the apostles each took "a coworker as wife."*

Paul also describes Andronicus and Junias, who had been imprisoned with him, as "outstanding among the apostles" (Romans 16:7). New Testament scholar Richard Bauckham says, "In this verse Paul almost certainly refers to two apostles, husband and wife, who engaged in traveling missionary work together as a two-person team. That they had at some point been in jail with Paul and were in Rome when Paul wrote shows that they were traveling missionaries, like Paul. . . . By calling Junias an apostle, Paul attributes to her the same authority as her husband and other male apostles, including Paul himself."†

Clement of Alexandria, one of the church fathers, says that the apostles' wives accompanied them "as co-ministers . . . in dealing with housewives. It was through them that the Lord's teaching penetrated also the women's quarters without any scandal being aroused."§ Bauckham says that in the Jewish society of the time, women and men were segregated much of the time, and at home, many women were confined to women's quarters. He adds, "[This] would limit the extent to which male missionaries could speak to women except when preaching in synagogue, and would also severely limit the possibilities of missionary work by women to men. It seems plausible that, within these social restrictions, a husband-

---

* Richard Bauckham, *Gospel Women: Studies of the Named Women in the Gospels* (Grand Rapids: William B. Eerdmans Publishing Company, 2002), 214, 215.

† Ibid., 215.

§ Quoted in ibid., 217.

and-wife missionary team would find it easier to reach both sexes with the gospel."*

Husband-and-wife church planting teams have played a vital role in the Seventh-day Adventist Church too.† Pastor E. B. and Mrs. E. S. Lane, for example, traveled throughout northeastern American states holding tent meetings. In 1875, Mrs. Lane spoke on health and temperance in Milford, New Hampshire, and by request, repeated the lecture in the town hall to a thousand people.

In 1876, the Lanes, with Pastor John Corliss and his wife, started the first Adventist congregation in the state of Virginia. In the summer of that year, in a thriving farming region near New Market, Mrs. Lane spoke to a group of several hundred people. It was reported, "Mrs. Lane is holding prayer meetings from house to house, to get the young and others into the work of praying and speaking in meeting. She has had excellent success." In another series of meetings she spoke to 650 people in a tent pitched on a Virginia farm.

In 1881, Pastor E. B. Lane died while conducting meetings in Camden, Michigan. His wife learned of his death while she was preaching elsewhere. Mrs. Lane continued her ministry for many years and in 1881 was granted a ministerial license.

Bert Haloviak, director of the Archives and Statistics department at the General Conference, writes, "She was a member of the ministerial association, attended minister's Bible Schools, led out in quarterly meetings, preached evangelistic sermons on all phases of denominational teaching, lectured to large . . . audiences on health and temperance matters, conducted revival meetings, made pastoral visits to languishing churches."

Lulu Wightman planted churches throughout New York State in Hornellsville, Gas Springs, Wallace, Silver Creek, Geneva, Angola, Gorham, Fredonia, Avoca, Rushville, Canandaigua, and Penn

---

* Ibid.

† The information in this section comes from Bert Haloviak's seminar "Women and the Adventist Church," presented at Sligo Adventist Church, October 15, 1988. It's available online at http://www.adventiststatistics.org.

Yan. She was considered by some as the "most successful minister in New York State between 1896 and 1905." Pastor S. M. Cobb wrote to the president of the New York Conference, "She has accomplished more the last two years than any minister in this state."

"Injustice has been done to women who labor just as devotedly as their husbands," wrote Ellen White, "and who are recognized by God as being as necessary to the work of ministry as their husbands" (Ms. 43a, 1898).

## Mission today

The young woman was short, dressed in black, with long dark hair, and standing in front of the largest Seventh-day Adventist church building I've seen. Surprisingly, it was in China in a city I won't name.

Every Sabbath more than three thousand people worship there, and in the surrounding district several thousand more worship in house churches. Through a translator I quickly learned that she was the church's pastor/leader and had started this church from a group of just eight people.

Slowly the story unfolded. This pastor began planting the church when she was in her early twenties. Now it has one of the largest, if not the largest, membership of any Seventh-day Adventist church in the world.

In a meeting room at the back of the church, I spoke through a translator with a group of fifty of this church's leaders, all enthusiastic and eager to learn. But I knew I was the one who needed to learn.

How could this church have happened? In a country with significant religious restrictions, here was a huge church with the Seventh-day Adventist logo prominently displayed on the front.

I later heard a story about this leader's dedication. In the early stages, when there was no Adventist church in the area, this young woman walked many miles to teach the Bible in someone's home. All evening she explained the Scriptures to the people gathered. As it neared 10:00 P.M., the time when the last bus would return to the city, she kept sharing. They were hungry to hear the Word of God but urged her not to miss the bus. Still she kept teaching.

Later, having missed the bus, she finally bid the group farewell. She continued walking through the night and early hours of the morning until she reached another home, where she conducted another Bible study. She hadn't had one moment's sleep but joyfully opened the Bible again.

This young woman is the most successful church planter I've met. Of course, this shouldn't surprise anyone. As the apostle Paul says, "There is neither Jew nor Greek, slave nor free, male nor female, for you are all one in Christ Jesus" (Galatians 3:28). All God's children, men and women, are called to be ministers of hope.

# CHAPTER 11

# Daniel and Friends: Dare to Have a Purpose Firm

Some years ago my wife, Bettina, brought home a special issue of the student newspaper from the Australian university where she was studying. It featured the upcoming student elections and listed the major groups and candidates running for office.

There were plenty to choose from—some serious, some not. They included The Green Alliance, an antinuclear group, Students Against Racism, The Left Alliance, a group called Dicing with the Devil, and even a party calling itself the O. J. Simpson Liberation Front.

But the group that caught my attention had only two candidates—Sean and Damien. Their group was the Actionless Party. All the other parties ran pictures of their candidates, but the Actionless Party candidates didn't show their faces. The spaces for their mug shots contained only these words: NO PHOTO SUPPLIED.

Sean's policy statement read, "As candidates for the Actionless Party, we promise to make no speeches, put up no posters, and publish no brochures. We promise not to attend any student council meetings and make no decisions. Some groups have been next to useless. Vote for us, and we will be exactly useless."

Damien wrote, "Most of the other candidates in this election believe they can make a difference. We, on the other hand, suffer no such illusions. Further, as a student of this university for five years, I've clearly demonstrated my ability to do absolutely nothing."

It seems to me that many Christians are members of the Spiritual Actionless Party. They're content to just drift along and never try too hard to advance God's kingdom.

In 606 B.C. four young Jewish men—Daniel (Belteshazzar), Hananiah (Shadrach), Mishael (Meshach), and Azariah (Abednego)—were among the first group of exiles taken from Judah to Babylon. It would have been the easiest thing in the world for them to forget their religious heritage and just merge into the culture and practices of Babylon. Banished as they were from home base and the spiritual support it provided, corporate worship with fellow Jews was only a memory. How painless just to drift into the Babylonian chapter of the Spiritual Actionless Party!

But if they felt any temptation in that direction, they firmly resisted. As the chorus of Philip Bliss's old hymn says:

> Dare to be a Daniel,
> Dare to stand alone!
> Dare to have a purpose firm!
> Dare to make it known.

The Babylonians brutally snatched these four young men from their families and homes and forced them to live in enemy territory hundreds of miles away. Babylon was a dreaded place—where people didn't know the Scriptures and worshiped false gods. How did Daniel and his three young friends stand by a "purpose firm"? How did they "dare to make it known" when threatened with death? Why do those of us in much easier circumstances today often waver in the face of temptation and avoid opportunities to stand for our faith?

## Exiled to Babylon

During the reign of King Jehoiakim of Judah, King Nebuchadnezzar of Babylon besieged Jerusalem. He pillaged the city, including the sacred temple, and herded Jews like cattle back to Babylon. Nebuchadnezzar ordered Ashpenaz, chief of his court officials, to select the elite of the young captives to serve in his palace. Daniel, Shadrach, Meshach, and Abednego were chosen for the king's court.

Just a few years earlier, King Josiah of Judah had restored the forgotten teachings of the prophets. But after his death, the people again fell into apostasy. Yet not all Judeans forgot God and His commandments. Faithful followers still trained their children in the paths they should go. That training would be tested in the lives of these four young Jewish exiles.

Over the centuries, Jewish prophets called their people to stay faithful to God and to be separate from pagan nations. God forbade intermarriage with people from other nations because it would open the floodgates to idolatry and apostasy. We often concentrate on the failures of God's people and overlook the fact that many stayed true despite horrific persecutions.

Almost four hundred fifty years after the time of Daniel, Greek ruler Antiochus Epiphanes sent a representative to Antioch to "compel the Jews to depart from the laws of their fathers and of God. And to defile the temple that was in Jerusalem and to call it the temple of Jupiter Olympius." According to the second book of Maccabees, "very bad was this invasion of evils and grievous to all" because pagan temples were full of all kinds of corrupt practices, including sexual promiscuity. Despite the threats, many Jews refused to compromise.

They were forced to wear ivy crowns during the feast to Bacchus and to perform sacrifices to pagan gods. Whoever refused was put to death. Two Jewish women who defied authorities by circumcising their sons were thrown headfirst over the city walls while still breastfeeding. A group of Jews escaped to nearby caves to keep the Sabbath secretly. They were discovered and burned to death.*

When Daniel and his friends reached Babylon, they were placed under the instruction of skilled teachers. For the first time they faced a worldview that was anathema to their Jewish tradition. The Babylonians didn't worship Yahweh. They didn't conform to Jewish dietary laws. They didn't keep the commandments. Biblical scholar Tremper Longman writes, "Archeological discoveries have revealed the curriculum for 'wise men' in this period of time. Besides the

---

* 2 Maccabees 6:2–11, http://www.drbo.org/chapter/46006.htm.

pagan creation and flood stories, the bulk of their education (after learning the incredibly difficult Akkadian language) would have been divination texts. They studied how to tell the future by watching the stars, pouring oil into water, reading omens from the livers of sheep, and many other ways."*

Suddenly thrust into the powerful and luxurious Babylonian court, how would they maintain their daily spiritual practices which, though so meaningful to them, didn't even register on the Babylonian radar?

This dilemma has challenged God's followers throughout history. When thrust from your home into an environment hostile to your beliefs and practices, how do you remain faithful? How can you effectively witness?

The three angels' messages of Revelation warn that Babylon has fallen, and the theme continues in Revelation 18:

> With a mighty voice he shouted:
>
> "Fallen! Fallen is Babylon the Great!
>     She has become a home for demons
> and a haunt for every evil spirit,
>     a haunt for every unclean and detestable bird.
> For all the nations have drunk
>     the maddening wine of her adulteries.
> The kings of the earth committed adultery with her,
>     and the merchants of the earth grew rich from her
>         excessive luxuries" (verses 2, 3).

Here the ancient city of Babylon symbolizes all that opposes the City of God, Jerusalem. It's the city of sin, apostasy, and every form of degradation. The message is clear: "Come out of her, my people, that ye be not partakers of her sins" (verse 4, KJV).

---

* Tremper Longman, "Graduating From Babylonian U—With Honors," *Christianity Today,* November 2007 (Web only), http://www.christianitytoday.com/ct/2007/novemberweb-only/147-22.0.html.

Far from Jerusalem, in the heart of Babylon, these Jewish young men couldn't "come out of her," but they did remain separate. Many years later Jesus would pray that His followers would be in the world but not of the world. Daniel and his friends were in Babylon, but not of it. They kept witness to the one true God.

Nearly three hundred years earlier, in the time of Elisha the prophet, Israel was constantly fighting border skirmishes with Syria. From that time comes a story Jesus quoted when He stood to teach for the first time in the Nazareth synagogue (Luke 4:27).

In one of their raids into Israel, Syrians captured a young Jewish girl and made her servant to the wife of Naaman, "commander of the army of the king of Aram" (2 Kings 5:1). Naaman was great, honorable, proud, and a mighty warrior. But one shocking fact undercut all his wealth, power, and position—he had leprosy, the most dreaded of diseases.

Thrown into the home of the military leader of Israel's enemy, the "little maid" must have been intimidated. How would they treat her? How would she know what to do and say? What dangers would she face? Would she be allowed to pray? How would she keep the Sabbath?

And yet that little girl became a missionary in a pagan household. Somehow she found the courage to testify to the power of the prophet Elisha. " 'I wish my master would go to see the prophet in Samaria,' " she said to her mistress one day. " 'He would heal him of his leprosy' " (verse 3, NLT).

She gave a bold testimony on several levels. First, although just a servant girl, she initiated the conversation. Second, she suggested that this powerful military leader should go to an enemy country for help. Third, she was taking a risk. What would happen if he wasn't healed? How could she be so confident? Although she knew Elisha was a miracle worker, there were no reports of him ever healing a leper. Even worse, what would happen if Naaman were ambushed and attacked while in Israel?

Yet her spiritual strength and character held firm. Her faith wasn't bound by geography or circumstances, and it empowered her to witness in the heart of enemy territory.

I attended Seventh-day Adventist schools through high school. When I enrolled at a secular university, I joined classes where my fellow students weren't Christians. I was a strict vegetarian, had never touched a drop of alcohol, was allergic even to the smell of cigarette smoke, and wouldn't have recognized a joint if I saw one. Now I was surrounded by people whose daily lives included all these and more.

I'll never forget the first day of one of my philosophy classes. The lecturer, Professor Robinson, was plump and bearded. He stood to introduce himself. He said that he used to be a preacher in the Methodist Church but was now an atheist. And then he paused, looked at us, and said sadly, "But I don't believe atheism needs any missionaries."

In his class, at least, I was spared direct attacks on Christianity. In other classes, I wasn't so fortunate. It's challenging to sit and listen to people more educated than you are criticize the very foundations of everything you've ever believed in.

At least I had a supportive Adventist family and a church I attended each week, where I felt as if I belonged. Daniel, Shadrach, Meshach, and Abednego had no support. We don't know if they even had any written Scriptures with them. Perhaps they could only cling to passages they'd memorized when growing up.

But the God in whom they trusted, whose teachings were ingrained in their lives, kept them faithful.

When we choose to follow God, we never know where He might send us or what He might ask us to do. These four young men may have been captives, but they were on a mission. They stood for truth and the true God and boldly witnessed for Him. It must have pleased God very much to see them share His love for His Babylonian children. After all, He is the God who longs for all people to know and serve Him (Isaiah 56:1–8).

Although God works in and through human history, this doesn't mean He's happy with everything that happens. Far from it. Free choice operates; and kings, governments, and citizens often defy God's will. But when He has willing agents, such as Daniel and his three friends, opportunities arise to advance His kingdom and its principles.

## Witness through lifestyle

The first major obstacle these young men faced was a buffet of royal food and wine, which they felt would "defile" them (Daniel 1:8). They proposed a different menu to the chief official, but he was skeptical. Although sympathetic, he said, " 'I am afraid of my lord, the king, who has assigned your food and drink. Why should he see you looking worse than the other young men your age? The king would then have my head because of you' " (verse 10).

But Daniel didn't give up. He asked the guard if they could have a trial period of ten days. After that time, the guard could compare their health with that of those following the king's diet. The guard agreed.

Of course, they proved healthier and better nourished than the other young men and impressed King Nebuchadnezzar with their wisdom and understanding.

Some time later, the king had a troubling dream that gave him insomnia. He probably tried having a hot drink, reading, or listening to music. But finally in the middle of the night, sick of counting sheep, he called all his "magicians, enchanters, sorcerers and astrologers" to interpret the dream (Daniel 2:2, 5).

" 'Tell your servants the dream,' " the wise men responded, " 'and we will interpret it' " (verse 4). But the king was insistent: describe the dream or die (verse 5). The astrologers panicked. " 'There is not a man on earth who can do what the king asks!' " they exclaimed (verse 10).

That wasn't the right answer. In his rage, the king ordered the execution of all Babylon's wise men. This immediately threatened Daniel and his friends (verse 13) because they, too, were considered "wise men" (verse 18).

After learning what was happening from Arioch, the commander of the king's guard, Daniel immediately went to the king and asked for time in order to interpret the dream. The king hadn't given this privilege to the other wise men, but he did so for Daniel. So Daniel gathered his three friends together for a prayer meeting (verses 17, 18), and God revealed the meaning of the dream. In thankfulness— and no doubt in great relief—Daniel praised Him (verse 19).

The next day Arioch took Daniel to the king, and Daniel recounted the dream and interpreted it. At the beginning and end of his speech, Daniel gave God credit (verses 28, 45). The explanation stunned Nebuchadnezzar, and he fell prostrate before Daniel. He also lavished gifts and honor on Daniel and promoted him in the royal court (verses 48, 49).

Ironically, this dream led to another test of faith. Nebuchadnezzar decided to memorialize his dream by erecting a huge golden statue and commanding his subjects to bow down and worship it. Shadrach, Meshach, and Abednego refused to bow—despite the threat of being burned alive.

Picture the scene. We don't know what the Babylonian climate was like back then, but if it was anything like modern-day Iraq, summer temperatures could soar above 120 degrees. No trees shaded the desert landscape of the Plain of Dura. Thousands gathered to bow before the golden statue that reached into the sky, shimmering in the heat.

Ellen White describes the Plain of Dura as a battleground between good and evil. "On that eventful day," she wrote, "the powers of darkness seemed to be gaining a signal triumph." She said that Satan wanted to permanently connect worship of the golden image with established idolatry to become the state religion in Babylon. "Satan hoped thereby," she added, "to defeat God's purpose of making the presence of captive Israel in Babylon a means of blessing to all the nations of heathendom" (Ellen G. White, *Prophets and Kings*, p. 506).

However, the victory was to be God's. First, the three young men gave a verbal testimony to the king: " 'O Nebuchadnezzar, we do not need to defend ourselves before you in this matter. If we are thrown into the blazing furnace, the God we serve is able to save us from it, and he will rescue us from your hand, O king. But even if he does not, we want you to know, O king, that we will not serve your gods or worship the image of gold you have set up' " (Daniel 3:16–18).

Shadrach, Meshach, and Abednego were confident that God could and would deliver them. They worshiped a God who could defy His own laws of physics and stop the fire from burning them. But the key words of this passage are "But even if he does not . . ." It's one thing to obey God when you know He'll save you. It's another thing to obey Him when there's a chance He won't.

"Our God is powerful enough to save us," they testified, "but if He chooses not to, we still won't worship your gods or golden image." Not only is the God they worship all-powerful, but He's totally trustworthy.

Can you imagine the reaction of the pagan officials surrounding the king? He was the greatest and most powerful being in their universe. He may not have had the power to create life, but he certainly had the power to take it away. When the king asked for their advice, they always told him what they thought he wanted to hear. When he told them to jump, they bowed and respectfully asked, "How high?" They scarcely breathed in his presence, let alone contradicted him. *And here were three young foreigners crassly defying him without hesitation.* Shadrach, Meshach, and Abednego stood firm. They were thrown into the furnace, yet not a hair of their heads was singed (verse 27)! As a result, Nebuchadnezzar praised their God and decreed that nobody could say anything against Him on pain of death (verses 28, 29). Nebuchadnezzar still had much to learn—including the beautiful truth that God doesn't enforce belief—but at least he was on the path to faith in the true God.

Once again these Jewish young men, through their faithfulness, advanced God's kingdom. Not only were they a testimony to the people of Babylon, but Ellen White says that "the tidings of their wonderful deliverance were carried to many countries by the representatives of the different nations that had been invited by Nebuchadnezzar to the dedication. Through the faithfulness of His children, God was glorified in all the earth" (*Prophets and Kings,* p. 512).

## Missionaries in Babylon
Nowhere in the book of Daniel do we see these Jewish young men knocking on doors, distributing leaflets, or running public-evangelism campaigns. These are all good things in their right place,

but Babylon wasn't the right place. Instead, the young men witnessed through their work, their decisions, their lives. Their witness flowed naturally from who they were and from their belief in, and commitment to, their God. Their spiritual commitment controlled every aspect of what they said and did. They refused to let the culture and expectations of the Babylonian state dictate their agenda. They refused to conform to decrees that attacked their beliefs and consciences.

They also made no effort to hide their religious practices. Later, the Persians conquered Babylon, and Nebuchadnezzar lost his throne. The new king, Darius, issued a vanity decree that anyone caught worshiping any god other than himself should be executed. Daniel didn't blink. He still opened his windows three times a day to face Jerusalem and pray to his God (Daniel 6:10). There was no hint of his drawing the blinds, finding a private place to pray, or even a quick "we're in a restaurant" type prayer. As a result, Daniel was thrown to the lions. But also as a result of his faith and deliverance, King Darius was led to belief in God (verses 26–28).

Today we all face Plains of Dura and lions' dens of various types. They're probably not as spectacular as those faced by Daniel and his three friends. But they may be just as important.

# CHAPTER 12

# Philip: Making Room for Eunuchs

I once spoke to chaplains meeting at Scott Air Force Base outside St. Louis, Missouri. After undergoing rigorous security checks, I asked directions to where the meetings were to be held.

I found the chapel and drove into the parking lot. The first space was clearly marked "Handicapped." I drove on.

The second space was marked "Handicapped." I drove on.

The third space also said "Handicapped." I drove on.

The fourth space said "General." *General!* I thought. *Great, that must be for everyone!* So I pulled in.

I was about to turn off the engine when it suddenly hit me that, on a military base, "General" has a specific and important meaning. I quickly reversed, half-listening for a guided missile headed my direction.

Have you ever felt you were in the wrong place? Somewhere you didn't fit in? Somewhere you didn't belong? How do we know where God wants us to be?

At the time Philip and six others were appointed deacons, the early church was suffering growing pains. The twelve apostles had been leading the growing group of believers, shepherding them in their new faith. They had wonderful times of harmony: "All the believers were one in heart and mind. No one claimed that any of his possessions was his own, but they shared everything they had. . . .

111

Much grace was upon them all" (Acts 4:32, 33). "They . . . ate together with glad and sincere hearts, praising God and enjoying the favor of all the people" (Acts 2:46, 47).

But difficulties soon arose, as they always seem to do when two or three humans gather. Quickly realizing they couldn't care for all the administration needed in the growing church, the apostles established a second tier of leadership—deacons.

We face a similar challenge today. Sabbath worship can lift us to the mountaintops of spiritual experience. But come Monday the church has to be cleaned, lawns mowed, bills paid. The church may be a spiritual community, but it exists on a real earth where we need to care for practical matters. We have to balance our spiritual mission with day-to-day "housekeeping."

Today we still ordain deacons to serve the church. But we often forget it's a spiritual calling, not just collecting the offering and organizing work bees. Deacons are spiritual leaders who perform administrative and pastoral duties. While he was performing this role, Philip was also learning to become an evangelist.

Stephen was one of the other seven deacons ordained with Philip. Luke describes him as "a man full of God's grace and power" (Acts 6:8). He died as the church's first martyr—stoned to death for his faith. This signaled the start of an intense persecution of the early church, and believers quickly scattered from Jerusalem. Philip fled to Samaria, where God gave him the gifts of healing and evangelism. Philip, the deacon, became Philip, the evangelist (Acts 21:8). In the midst of dreadful persecution, the apostle Paul's promise was demonstrated once again: "And we know that all things work together for good to them that love God, to them who are the called according to his purpose" (Romans 8:28, KJV). Although God didn't plan the persecution, which must have grieved Him, He created good from bad—the gospel spread throughout Samaria and other areas where believers had escaped.

Philip may have been a wonderful preacher, but miracles were his entering wedge. Luke writes, "When the crowds heard Philip and saw the miraculous signs he did, they all paid close attention to

112

what he said" (Acts 8:6). People listened to him because he cast out evil spirits and healed the paralyzed and lame.

Yet miracles had their limitations. A few years earlier, Jesus had been reluctant to show miraculous signs (see, for example, Mark 8:12; Luke 11:29). Of course, He still performed miracles, but as an essential part of His holistic ministry, not to prove He was the Messiah. He knew miracles are poor evidence of God. People hunger for the supernatural, but often they quickly run to the next and best magician or miracle worker—without ever changing their lives.

## Simon Magus

Philip encountered a prominent "miracle worker," Simon Magus, in Samaria. Through his magic and witchcraft, Simon had built up a major following. He boasted of his own greatness, and people idolized him, blasphemously saying, " 'This man is the divine power known as the Great Power' " (Acts 8:10). But after witnessing Philip's superior miracles and hearing his riveting message, Simon's followers turned to Jesus and were baptized. Surprisingly, Simon himself also believed and was baptized.

After his baptism, Simon continued to follow Philip and was dazzled by the signs and wonders he performed (verse 13). Simon fixated on the glamour of miracles, but his life didn't change. His superficial conversion had the potential to seriously undermine the new group of believers in Samaria.

When the leaders in Jerusalem heard about the wonderful things God was doing in Samaria, they sent Peter and John, the most experienced apostles, to visit. After arriving, they encountered the notorious Simon.

Simon watched Peter and John pray for new believers to receive the Holy Spirit. Again he was impressed. This could be a wonderful new addition to his list of magic tricks. He offered the apostles money for the power to bestow the Holy Spirit on people (verses 18, 19). Peter and John were outraged. " 'May your money be destroyed with you for thinking God's gift can be bought!' " Peter thundered (verse 20, NLT).

Early Christian writings brand Simon Magus as a heretic and one of the early leaders of Gnosticism, a spiritual movement trading in so-called secret knowledge. According to Ellen White, Simon later followed Peter to Rome "to oppose and hinder the work of the gospel." There he enjoyed patronage from the emperor Nero. When Peter exposed Simon's deception, Nero became angry and jailed Peter (see Ellen G. White, *Sketches From the Life of Paul*, p. 328).

## The Ethiopian eunuch

Despite his problems with Simon, Philip was enjoying great success in Samaria when suddenly an angel gave him a new assignment. "The last thing an evangelist wants to do is leave town when everybody is answering the altar call!" someone once said. But Philip immediately obeyed.

The angel sent Philip to the road connecting Jerusalem to Gaza (a distance of some fifty miles). On his way, he saw an Ethiopian eunuch traveling to Ethiopia—a territory roughly corresponding with today's Sudan. The eunuch was returning from Jerusalem to which he'd traveled probably full of hope at the prospect of worshiping at the temple.

Now on his way home, the eunuch was reading aloud from the book of Isaiah. Words on parchment scrolls had no spaces between them and no punctuation; the letters ran to the edges of the scroll. The best way to understand what you were reading was to read aloud—sounding out each word from the long line of letters.

Prompted by the Holy Spirit, Philip ran close to the eunuch, heard what he was reading, and asked him if he understood it. " 'How can I,' " the eunuch said, " 'unless someone explains it to me?' " (verse 31). So he asked Philip to ride next to him and explain the puzzling passage. Philip didn't need a second invitation.

Providentially, the eunuch was reading from one of the Bible's most beautiful descriptions of Jesus' sacrifice. It was the launching pad for Philip to teach the Ethiopian the good news about Jesus— exactly what he needed to hear.

No doubt he was returning home discouraged. Perhaps depressed. On two counts he wouldn't have been welcome at the

Jerusalem temple—as a eunuch and as a Gentile (clearly shown by his black skin). Jewish tradition banished eunuchs from the "assembly of the Lord" (Deuteronomy 23:1). And no Gentiles of any description were allowed into the temple to worship.

An inscription on the temple wall separating the Court of the Gentiles from the Court of the Jews threatened death to any Gentile who dared cross into the other court. It wasn't a warm welcome. The Imperial New Museum in Istanbul, Turkey, houses an inscribed stone from Herod's temple in Jerusalem. Discovered in 1871, it reads: "No outsider shall enter the protective enclosure around the sanctuary. And whoever is caught will have only himself to blame for his ensuing death."*

When Paul wrote that Jesus has broken down "the wall of hostility that separated us [Jews and Gentiles]" (Ephesians 2:14, NLT), he was probably thinking about the two courts in the temple. Now Philip demonstrated the truth of Paul's words by extending Christian fellowship to a Gentile eunuch. It was a day God had waited a long time for. Back in the time of the prophet Isaiah God had said, " 'And my blessings are also for the eunuchs. They are as much mine as anyone else' " (Isaiah 56:3, NLT).

In Jesus' last recorded words to His disciples, He said, " 'You will receive power and will tell people about me everywhere—in Jerusalem, throughout Judea, in Samaria, and to the ends of the earth' " (Acts 1:8, NLT). Philip had helped spread the good news throughout Samaria. And now from one of the "ends of the earth," the first African—possibly the first Gentile—accepts the good news and joins the Christian church.

The eunuch continued home to Africa, the first missionary to his own people. According to the early church fathers, this eunuch established the church in Ethiopia that gave rise to influential church leaders such as Clement of Alexandria and Origen.

Today we don't have church rules banning eunuchs from worshiping with us. It's not an issue. But are there any modern-day

---

* Translation by K. C. Hanson and Douglas E. Oakman, http://www.kchanson .com/ANCDOCS/greek/templewarning.html.

equivalents of eunuchs whom we find it difficult to welcome into our fellowship?

The story is told about a man arriving at the Pearly Gates and being greeted by Peter.*

"Did I really make it?" the man asked.

"Yes," replied St. Peter, "you sure did. But before you can enter, you must do one more thing."

"What's that?" asked the man.

"Spell a word," Peter replied.

"What word?"

"Any word," answered Peter. "It's your choice."

"Well," said the man, "the word I'll spell is *love.* L-o-v-e."

"Congratulations," said Peter. "You're in."

A few moments later Peter asked the newest citizen of heaven if he would be so kind as to take his place at the gates for a few minutes. The man was delighted to help.

But a few moments later he was shocked to see his mother-in-law arriving. The thought of spending eternity with her sent chills up his spine.

Through gritted teeth he greeted her, and she asked, "Did I really make it to heaven?"

"Not yet," he replied. "You must first spell a word."

"What word?" she asked.

The man thought long and hard before responding.

*"Czechoslovakia,"* he said.

Do we sometimes act like this man standing at the gates of heaven, obstructing people trying to get in? Or are we like Philip, opening our arms to all people, no matter what their background or the label around their neck?

## Do you understand what you are reading?

I once had an experience the reverse of Philip's. I didn't ask someone about what she was reading; someone asked me what I was reading. And it wasn't on a chariot; it was on a plane.

---

* In case anyone had any doubt, this is a parable telling a story that did not happen.

I was returning from Orlando, Florida, to Washington, D.C., and reading my Bible. An hour into the flight, the young woman sitting next to me suddenly interrupted and said, "Are you reading that thing right through like a novel?"

I looked down at my open Bible, where I'd been quietly working my way through 2 Chronicles.

"Yes, I guess I am," I replied.

"Why?"

"I read the Bible through every January. It makes a good start to the year."

She then described her husband's bad start with Christianity thanks to strict fundamentalist parents. Cruelty and hypocrisy turned him away, and now he had no time for church. "Neither of us are Christians," she said.

"And then," she added, catching her breath, "my mother's gone and become one of those Seventh-day Adventists!"

She had my attention. I listened closely as she proceeded to describe my church family—"very strange people," "vegans," "sunken eyes," "anorexic-looking." She shook her head and circled her ear with her finger. "You know how the [she named another religious group] always come knocking on your door?"

"Yes," I replied, tentatively.

"My mother's the only person I know who has *them* wanting to leave."

Many good Christians pray for witnessing opportunities when they travel. If this was an opportunity, I wish it were packaged more attractively. I was tempted to take the safe course and say, "Yeah, how about those Adventists? Crazy, aren't they?" and return piously to my Bible.

Generally, the last thing I want on a plane is a long conversation with the person next to me. Especially when we've still got a long way to go and you know she's going to be thinking the whole way, *This guy belongs to a bunch of weirdos.* But I took the plunge. As I broke the news that I, too, was a Seventh-day Adventist, I tried to do it gently.

For the rest of the flight I discussed spiritual things with this young woman and her young university-student friend, who had the window seat. Neither believed the Bible, and they both had a long list of questions. When we arrived in Washington, I felt I hadn't accomplished much. But as we landed, her friend handed me a pen and asked me to write down the translation of the Bible I was reading. She wanted to look at the Bible for herself.

Neither of those girls asked me to baptize them. But perhaps a seed was sown. God may not supernaturally transport us, like Philip, from place to place to witness for Him. But He opens up avenues wherever we're located.

I stood up to get my bags from the overhead compartment and noticed the back of my shirt was soaking wet. I'd been sweating my way through their questions. I hadn't found it easy trying to answer questions to which there aren't easy answers.

Biblical stories sometimes make it sound easy, and Philip's life appears to be one of miracle after miracle. But perhaps as he ran up to that high-ranking official in the chariot, even Philip may have had some misgivings. Perhaps he was nervous. I don't know. But I like to think he might have sweated a bit.

Certainly, it wasn't all triumph. Simon Magus seemingly accepted Jesus, but his life wasn't changed, and he went on to menace the church. And perhaps there were other times when Philip witnessed and people didn't respond. Certainly that was Jesus' own experience. God calls us to be missionaries, but He doesn't guarantee 100 percent success.

## It's an adventure

Whatever happens, following Jesus is always an adventure. It's never predictable and risk-free. Each year, many Civil War sites in the United States host reenactments of famous battles. It's amazing how organizers and participants make everything as authentic as possible. They thoroughly research the battles, planning all the correct formations. They dress in proper union and confederate uniforms. They carry muskets and fire canons. It's all realistic, but, of course, nobody gets killed—which is a good thing all round.

Søren Kierkegaard, the Danish philosopher, describes a mock battle just like these. He says the battle cry sounds, the muskets fire, and cannons thunder. It looks like a real battle. It sounds like a real battle. It smells like a real battle. Except for one thing. There's something missing. There's no danger. It's only pretend.

So it is, said Kierkegaard, with "playing Christianity." People attend church Sunday morning in their best clothes. They perform all the rituals, and they leave unchanged. It looks like Christianity. It sounds like Christianity. But one thing's missing. There's no danger.*

In the famous faith chapter in Hebrews we read about people who followed God and "conquered kingdoms," "administered justice," "shut the mouths of lions," "quenched the fury of the flames," "escaped the edge of the sword," "became powerful in battle" (Hebrews 11:33, 34).

But it all came with risk. The passage continues to say that others were "tortured," "jeered at, and their backs were cut open with whips," "chained in prisons." Some "died by stoning," "were sawed in half," were "killed with the sword," were "hungry and oppressed and mistreated." As the writer says, "They were too good for this world" (verses 35–38, NLT).

Philip personally saw the danger of following Jesus when his friend and fellow deacon, Stephen, was killed. Perhaps in the roller-coaster adventure of his life there were times when he questioned God's leading and wondered where he should go and what he should do. But ultimately Philip discovered that when he went where God sent him, it was always the best place to be.

---

* Søren Kierkegaard, translated by Walter Lowrie, *Attack Upon Christendom* (Princeton, N.J.: Princeton University Press, 1968), 180.

# CHAPTER 13

# Isaiah: False Teeth and Bombs

On July 7, 2007, more than a hundred musicians on seven continents performed a series of concerts to highlight the environmental threat of global warming. Concert-goers joined an estimated television audience of two billion.

Cynics called it a stunt, and even some performers doubted they would change anything. "I'm not a scientist," said singer Dave Matthews. "I'm not saying we can save the planet. But we might as well grab for straws before we go down, you know?"*

But optimism reigned. The twenty-four-hour event concluded at the eighty-thousand-seat Giants Stadium in New Jersey, United States, with the British group, The Police, singing:

> I'll send an S.O.S. to the world
> I hope that someone gets my . . .
> Message in a bottle, yeah!

During the song, rapper Kanye West joined the band and out of nowhere began yelling over and over, "We can save the world! We can save the world! We can save the world!"† It was a fairly ambi-

---

\* David Green, "Live Earth: The Music and the Message," http://www.npr.org/templates/story/story.php?storyId=11813655.

† John Pareles, "A Global Chorus on Climate Change," *The New York Times,* July 8, 2007.

tious way to end the day. It was also an odd thing for West, a self-confessed follower of Jesus, to claim. Even if we conquer climate change, we haven't saved the world.

## Saving the world

Throughout history God has sent prophets as human agents in His plan to save the world. In the Scriptures, prophet vacancies weren't posted in help-wanted ads. It wasn't a position you could apply for (God didn't tolerate self-appointed prophets—see Jeremiah 14:14; 23:21).

The Hebrew word for "prophet," *nabi,* means "mouthpiece" or "interpreter" of God. The job description sounds impressive, but it had its drawbacks. Prophets were regularly scorned, attacked, jailed, tortured, and killed. Jeremiah was beaten and put in stocks (Jeremiah 20:1, 2). Zechariah was stoned to death (2 Chronicles 24:21). Their job wasn't to massage the ears of their audience with happy words. It was to deliver messages from God—whether good news or bad, whether people wanted to hear or not.

Although dramatically called as a prophet, Isaiah didn't feel adequate. Confronted by a vision of the Divine, he immediately confessed his sin and confessed his unworthiness. A seraphim took a live coal from the heavenly altar, touched it to Isaiah's mouth, and said, " 'See, this has touched your lips; your guilt is taken away and your sin atoned for' " (Isaiah 6:7). Isaiah had confessed, and God could now use him. He was spiritually prepared.

God never calls anyone for service without equipping him or her. When the angel appeared to Mary, she was troubled and afraid (Luke 1:29, 30). She seemed poorly qualified to be the mother of Jesus—" 'How will this be,' Mary asked the angel, 'since I am a virgin?' " (Luke 1:34). The angel settled the question—" 'Nothing is impossible with God' " (verse 37).

God purified Isaiah's unclean lips (see Isaiah 6:7), gave Mary the Holy Spirit and " 'the power of the Most High' " (Luke 1:35), gave speechless Moses a spokesperson (Exodus 4:14–16), and inserted words into Jeremiah's mouth (Jeremiah 1:9). Jesus prayed for Peter (Luke 22:32) and anointed Saul with the Holy Spirit (Acts 9:17, 18).

But let's remember the difference between what we need and what we might want. When God called Abraham to leave Ur, He didn't provide a map and a detailed travel schedule. He didn't provide first-class airline seats with lacto-ovo vegetarian meals, in-flight movies, and frequent flyer points. He called Abraham on an adventure. Like Isaiah, Abraham was prepared to follow God's command without knowing where he was headed.

When Jesus called the fishermen beside Galilee, He didn't offer a job interview to discuss their new careers. He didn't talk to them about pay rates, vacation time, retirement programs, child-care provisions, and other employee benefits. Jesus called them on an adventure.

When Isaiah heard God ask, " 'Whom shall I send, and who will go for us?' " (Isaiah 6: 8), he replied, " 'Here am I. Send me.' " He didn't think he was the best person for the job. The task wasn't so attractive that he couldn't resist (he didn't even know what the task was). He accepted the invitation because he knew that although he was unworthy, God was worthy. Although Isaiah was powerless, God was powerful. Isaiah didn't choose the mission; God did.

Isaiah's primary message was salvation for the world. God had chosen Israel as a servant nation to follow His laws and to bring other nations back to Him. So many times Israel failed its mission. Rather than being a witness, it often compromised with other nations. Isaiah tried valiantly to bring Israel back on track and to cast a vision of the light of truth going out from Israel to all Gentile nations.

God's plans stretched further than the people imagined. Sure, He wanted to see warring tribes of Judah and Israel reconciled. But that was only a first step. " 'It is too small a thing for you to be my servant to restore the tribes of Jacob and bring back those of Israel I have kept,' " He said (Isaiah 49:6). In other words, God's vision included more than just Israel. " 'I will also make you a light for the Gentiles, that you may bring my salvation to the ends of the earth.' "

Isaiah prophesied that one day there would be "an altar to the Lord in the heart of Egypt" (19:19). This was almost incomprehensible. "In Isaiah's day there was no other nation on earth that was so much in the grip of superstition and filthy idolatry as Egypt," writes Dutch author Harry Bultema. "Apes, cats, frogs, crocodiles, lizards—everything was venerated by them."* Yet Isaiah devoted his life to that day when not only would Egypt turn to God, but the Egyptians would join with the murderous Assyrians in worshiping God: "The Assyrians will go to Egypt and the Egyptians to Assyria. The Egyptians and Assyrians will worship together. In that day Israel will be the third, along with Egypt and Assyria, a blessing on the earth" (verses 23, 24).

" 'And my blessings are for Gentiles, too, when they commit themselves to the Lord,' " God added. " 'Do not let them think that I consider them second-class citizens' " (Isaiah 56:3, NLT).

God chose Israel as His special instrument, but that didn't mean He loved or cared for them more than He did other nations. All were His children. There are no "second-class citizens" as far as God's salvation is concerned.

## Sick of ritual

In the opening chapter of Isaiah, God says religious ritual wearies Him: " 'I have more than enough of burnt offerings.' " " 'Your incense is detestable to me.' " " 'Your New Moon festivals and your appointed feasts my soul hates' " (Isaiah 1:11–14). The book of Amos echoes this theme. " 'I hate, I despise your religious feasts; I cannot stand your assemblies' " (Amos 5:21).

Several hundred years later Jesus continued this prophetic theme, condemning the Pharisees for following ritual and ignoring its meaning. " 'Woe to you, teachers of the law and Pharisees, you hypocrites!' " He said. " 'You give a tenth of your spices—mint, dill and cummin' " (Matthew 23:23).

The Pharisees were strict. They went to their gardens and tithed every ounce of everything they grew—even the herbs. " 'But,' " Jesus added, " 'you have neglected the more important matters of the law—justice, mercy and faithfulness. You should have practiced the latter, without neglecting the former.' " To drive home His point, Jesus added, " 'You blind guides! You strain out a gnat but swallow a camel' " (verse 24).

---

* "Isaiah 19—The Burden Against Egypt," quoted in http://www.enduringword.com/commentaries/2319.htm.

Gnats bite and annoy. But they're tiny. Insignificant. On the other hand, it's hard to ignore a camel. They're particularly hard to ignore in rutting season, when they can turn violent. They can injure or even kill with a well-placed kick. At the very least, they'll spit at you when they get upset. Jesus was saying, "You religious leaders have your priorities completely turned around the wrong way. Gnats may occasionally grab your attention, but they're nothing compared to large, spitting, stinking camels."

Toward the end of World War II, Japanese bombers attacked Darwin, in northern Australia. The city prepared for the worst. Authorities evacuated public buildings. The story is told that the city hospital's chief executive officer furiously rushed around checking that all staff and patients were out of the building. As he looked down his list, he saw that the matron wasn't accounted for. Heroically he dashed into the building to search for her. Sprinting from room to room, he finally found her rummaging through a chest of drawers.

"What are you doing?" he yelled. "Let's get out of here!"

"I'm looking for my false teeth," she replied.

"You're looking for what?"

"My false teeth. I've lost my false teeth."

"Get out of here," the CEO screamed. "They're dropping bombs, not sandwiches!"

Now, if you've lost your real teeth, false teeth can be a blessing. But they're not much use if a bomb lands on you. It's a question of priorities.

Too often we fumble around with false teeth while more important things are going on. Tithing is important. But it's nothing if we neglect justice, faithfulness, and mercy. Ritual can keep us focused, but it's a curse as an end in itself.

Isaiah knew this well. He appears to have had friends in high places and had free access to the royal palace. Some speculate that he must have belonged to the upper classes. But he was most concerned for those lower on the socioeconomic scale—the widows, orphans, foreigners, and the poor. " 'Learn to do right!' " he thunders. " 'Seek justice, encourage the oppressed. Defend the cause of the fatherless, plead the case of the widow' " (Isaiah 1:17).

Isaiah's words anticipate Jesus' priorities when He came to earth. Standing for the first time to speak in a synagogue, Jesus read from Isaiah, " 'The Spirit of the Lord is on me, because he has anointed me to preach good news to the poor. He has sent me to proclaim freedom for the prisoners and recovery of sight for the blind, to release the oppressed, to proclaim the year of the Lord's favor' " (Luke 4:18, 19).

This was Jesus' mission statement. He was looking out from the synagogue to a world where people were poor, imprisoned, blind, and oppressed.

Many Christians speak disparagingly of the "social gospel"—a gospel, they say, that is concerned only with humanitarian care and ignores "the spiritual." Certainly that's a danger. Can we be content with giving someone only a cup of water if they don't know about the Water of Life? But in an important sense the gospel is a social gospel. It's not just some intellectual knowledge; it changes the way we treat others. What use is the good news if it doesn't change people? Jesus revealed good news for all dimensions of our lives.

When Jesus separates the sheep from the goats at the end of time, His measure won't be some deep theological issue that has engaged the attention of the church's best scholars. The issues that separate are simple: " ' "I was hungry and you gave me something to eat, I was thirsty and you gave me something to drink, I was a stranger and you invited me in, I needed clothes and you clothed me, I was sick and you looked after me, I was in prison and you came to visit me" ' " (Matthew 25:35, 36).

According to Isaiah, it's not enough to call upon the name of the Lord and to perform religious rituals. God wants far more than that. He tells us to repent, " 'wash and make yourselves clean. Take your evil deeds out of my sight!' " (Isaiah 1:16), to live properly, and to care for the poor and oppressed, the orphans and the widows.

How could Israel teach other nations if it couldn't even look after its own needy? What sort of example was a nation that lacked business ethics and mistreated widows and orphans? For Isaiah, true religion in practice changed society. It compassionately worked for justice. It stood in judgment against those who professed to be religious but who ignored the poor and suffering.

## Hardening hearts

It must have frustrated Isaiah to share a clear message from God and to be totally ignored. It must have also frustrated God. At one stage He says to Isaiah, "Make the heart of this people fat, and make their ears heavy, and shut their eyes; lest they see with their eyes, and hear with their ears, and understand with their heart, and convert, and be healed" (Isaiah 6:10, KJV).

This seems odd—that God would want to blur people's understanding. But the problem is translation. Rather than stating what God would cause, the passage predicts what would happen despite His will. The Septuagint, an early Greek translation of the Old Testament, clarifies, "Ye shall hear indeed, but ye shall not understand; and ye shall see indeed, but ye shall not perceive. For the heart of this people has become gross, and their ears are dull of hearing, and their eyes have they closed; lest they should see with their eyes, and hear with their ears, and understand with their heart, and be converted, and I should heal them."*

Isaiah wanted to soften the people's hearts. But, as they rejected his warnings, their hearts naturally hardened.

I'll never forget some years ago visiting the remains of the Dachau concentration camp, in a peaceful suburban street on the outskirts of Munich, Germany. It sat beside a soccer field filled with the cries and laughter of children playing. It was such an ordinary scene. I wondered whether children had played on this field fifty years earlier, more interested in the next goal than the dark walls behind them.

Most of the camp's buildings were destroyed, but the walls, gates, and crematorium still stand as a chilling memorial.

I was fascinated to browse through a tourist brochure for the town. In it the mayor of Dachau welcomed visitors, "The horrors of the German concentration camps must never be repeated! After your visit, you will be horror-stricken. But we sincerely hope you will not transfer your indignation to the ancient 1200-year-old

---

* Translation by Sir Lancelot C. L. Brenton, 1851, online at http://www.ecmarsh.com/lxx/Esaias/Esaias%20LXX.htm.

Bavarian town of Dachau, which was not consulted when the concentration camp was built and whose citizens voted quite decisively against the rise of National Socialism in 1933."

The brochure added, "They [the Dachau citizens] didn't know the details of what was going on behind the walls of the camp." Could this really have been the case? How did they explain the thousands of people transported to Dachau and herded like cattle into the camp? But what about us Christians today? Have we erected walls around the church that block our view of what's happening in our community? Are we blind to those in need?

Danish philosopher Søren Kierkegaard describes a hospital where patients were dying like flies. Doctors panicked and scrambled for a cure. But nothing worked. Poison polluted the building.

So it was, said Kierkegaard, with the state church in Denmark. Congregations were dying, and everyone had a cure—a new hymn book, a different style of worship, a new altar book. But all was in vain. Spiritual poison emanated from the "building," suffocating the whole organization. The church hadn't been ventilated, spiritually, for years.*

In 1980, my good friend Bronwyn Reid was living in a commune of sorts in downtown Sydney, Australia. She and her friends "liberated" (to use her word) vacant government-owned buildings, moved in, and lived rent-free.

Their alternative lifestyle attracted artists, musicians, backpackers, hippies, and "assorted fringe dwellers" from a variety of ethnic backgrounds. "I was a young idealist, immersed in the counterculture world of New Age philosophies, yet not really convinced that these 'gurus' had the answers," she says.

Bronwyn had grown up in another denomination but left when she was a teenager. She now felt impressed to study the Bible for herself and chose to contact Adventists because she'd heard about their holistic lifestyle. Being a vegetarian, Bronwyn felt "a kindred spirit."

---

* Søren Kierkegaard, *Attack Upon Christendom* (Princeton, N.J.: Princeton University Press, 1991), 139, 140.

"With a searching heart and an open mind I nervously walked off the street and into my first Sabbath service," she says. "I sat at the back of the church, only to be informed by a somewhat intimidating woman that I was sitting in her reserved space. It was an interesting welcome."

Bronwyn recalls singing old hymns and listening to a sermon that contained words and phrases she'd never heard before, such as "the remnant," "Spirit of Prophecy," and "the three angels' messages." At the end, someone announced a free "record" available in the foyer and that there would be a potluck the following week.

As a musician, Bronwyn was keen to hear what was on the Adventist record. And as a dope-smoking hippie, she was kind of interested in what a "pot" luck might be. "After church I asked for this 'record,'" she recalls, "and was directed to a 'deaconess,' who stared me up and down and then told me that since I wasn't a church member, I wasn't entitled to receive one." Bronwyn went home wondering if being a Seventh-day Adventist required charisma-bypass surgery.

She later discovered that the *Record* was the church paper for the South Pacific Division of the Adventist Church and that Adventists don't smoke pot at a potluck (although there's still a high chance of getting poisoned).

"That first visit was a culture shock," Bronwyn says. "I was obviously different and felt like an outsider who didn't know the language and certainly didn't look the part. I seriously doubted whether the Adventist Church was a good place for me, and only my inner hunger to find truth kept me from giving up."*

How can we spiritually ventilate our churches? What's the antidote for spiritual poisoning? We need a fresh Isaiah vision of reaching the world with Jesus' love and compassion. We need to tear down those church doors and rip them off their hinges. We need to grasp the church windows and throw them wide open.

---

* Bronwyn Reid, "What on Earth Are We Doing?" *Adventist Review,* July 23, 1997, 11.